A History of

THE DEVONSHIRE ROYAL HOSPITAL AT BUXTON

and the Buxton Bath Charity

Mike Langham & Colin Wells

ACKNOWLEDGEMENTS

We are indebted to a number of people who have been associated with us in the production of this book. In recounting the 20th century history we have received important help and information from Rita Urion, Sue Allan, Myles Burgess, Jane Webster and Mr J.M. Laughton F.R.C.S. In architectural and technical matters we are fortunate to have been able to call upon Ian Deaville's comprehensive knowledge of the hospital and to meet with Dr Ron Fitzgerald and Allan Woodhead of Structural Perspectives, Halifax, who have stimulated valuable debate and given permission to use their work to inform this book. Rosie Hughes, in the campaign office of the University of Derby, has kept us up to date with developments at the hospital site and Professor Waterhouse has provided a most apposite foreword. We have received customary support from staff at the Buxton Library and the Museum & Art Gallery. Ian Clements has produced some excellent line drawings for us.

Some people have been closely involved with our research as it progressed; Michael Bryant has been generous in sharing with us knowledge gained in a career in physiotherapy at the hospital, and has been a particular help in reading and correcting the final draft. Trevor Gilman has been our personal technical consultant and, with his partner Margery Sherwood, has provided a contribution to the book on the High Peak Health Forum in chapter four. This is our sixth joint book and every one has been meticulously read in draft form by our good friend and local historian Oliver Gomersal and we thank him and his wife Marjorie for their unwavering support in all our work. Finally we should like to particularly thank Mrs Elizabeth Snow, great grand daughter of Robert Rippon Duke for providing us with original drawings and much other material relating to the Devonshire Hospital and the work of its architect. We thank them all and we consider ourselves fortunate to have such valuable friends and colleagues to help with this prominent aspect of the history of Buxton spa and inland resort.

We are grateful to the following organisations who have given us permission to use illustrations: Portrait of CW Buckley; Clinic physio room (59437) and Clinic Xray theatre (59438) from the Board Collection. The visit of Edward VII from the Museum Collections courtesy of Derbyshire County Council, Buxton Museum and Art Gallery. 1858 conversion, upper floor (D45081311112) and New baths 1914 (D45081112) from Derbyshire County Council, Derbyshire Record Office, Matlock. Plan of consulting rooms c. 1854, (Folder T Buxton Plans) Devonshire Mss., Chatsworth. Reproduced by permission of the Duke of Devonshire and the Chatsworth Settlement Trustees. Radio DRH from The Nursing Times. We thank the following friends who have loaned us material from their personal collections: Myles Burgess; Trevor Gilman; Keith Holford; Rod Leach - The Camerman for the cover. All other illustrations are from the authors' collections.

MJL and CW, Buxton, April 2003

CHURNET VALLEY BOOKS
1 King Street, Leek, Staffordshire. ST13 5NW 01538 399033
thebookshopleek.co.uk
© Mike Langham & Colin Wells and Churnet Valley Books 2003
ISBN 1 904546 02 1

Printed and bound by Bath Press

CONTENTS

EXPLANATORY NOTES ON MEASUREMENTS

Historically it is necessary to make descriptions using the units of measurement prevailing at the time. In order to bring such measurements up to date we give below a series of conversion tables and conversions of some of the more common measurements found in the book.

Temperature: Fahrenheit (F) was most frequently used in this country until decimalisation when Celsius (C) came into use. The formulae are: C = (F-32) x 0.55. F = 9 x C + 32.5. The temperature found commonly in the book is that of the Buxton Natural Mineral Water which emerges at 82°F or 27.5°C.

Currency: Imperial currency used pounds (£), shillings (s) and pence (d) where £1 = 20s. and 1s. = 12d. Upon decimalisation in 1971 the convention became pounds (£) and pence (p) where £1 = 100p.

Approximate conversions for some currency found in the book are:
8d. = 3p; 1s.= 5p; 2s. = 10p; 2s.6d. = 12p; 3s. 4d. = 17p; 4s. = 20p; 5s. = 25p; 6s. = 30p; 6s.8d. = 34p; 7s.6d. = 37p; 10s. = 50p; 13s. 4d. = 67p; 30s. = £1.50p; £2.12s.6d. = £2.62p; £3.10s. = £3.50p; 40s. = £2. One guinea was 21s. or £1.05p. 4 guineas (£4.4s.) = £4.20p; 5 guineas (£5.5s.) = £5.25p; 10 guineas (£10.10s.) = £10.50p; 15 guineas (£15.15s.) = £15.75p; 20 guineas = £21.

Measurement: Imperial measurement uses yards (yds.) feet (ft.) and inches where 12 inches = 1 ft. and 3ft. = 1 yd. The decimal system of linear measurement uses metres (m), centimetres (cm) and millimetres (mm) where 1m. = 100cm and 1cm = 10 mm. Common conversions are: 25mm = 1 inch.; 2.5cm = 1 inch.; 300mm. = 1ft.; 1m. = 3ft. 3inches or 39 inches.

Approximate conversions for some measurements in the book are:
5ft. 4 inches = 1.5m; 10ft = 3m; 13ft = 4m; 15ft = 4.6m; 17ft = 5.2m; 18ft = 5.5m; 20ft = 6.2m; 25ft = 7.7m; 26ft. 6 inches = 8m; 30ft. = 9.2m; 50ft. = 15.4m; 60ft. = 18.5m; 75ft. = 23m; 93ft. = 28.6m; 112ft. = 34.5m; 118ft. = 36.3m; 137ft. = 42.2m; 138ft. = 42.5m; 140ft. = 43m; 142ft. = 43.7m; 145ft. = 44.6m; 156ft. 6 inches = 48m; 164ft. = 50.5m.; 180ft. = 55.5m; 219ft. = 67.4m.

FOREWORD

By Professor Roger Waterhouse Vice-Chancellor of the University of Derby

The Devonshire Royal Hospital is a unique and wonderful building, a landmark for the community and a glory to the town. From the first it was associated with the development of tourism and the spa for which Buxton is so justly famous. The history of this remarkable piece of architecture is writ throughout the building, though most of us can read it only dimly without a guide. Entering into its splendid dome is an experience which cannot be captured on the printed page. It is truly awe inspiring.

The history of the building is not just about its stones and slates, its iron and lead. It is about the people who created it and the communities it served. Robert Rippon Duke (1817–1909) was architect to the Hospital during its most formative years. There could be no better people than Mike Langham and Colin Wells, his biographers, and intrepid researchers into Buxton's history, to tell the story of the people and the building.

The Devonshire Royal Hospital brought healing to sufferers from rheumatism and arthritis for nearly 150 years. The numbers of patients and carers throughout that period were legion. There are still many many people who remember the Devonshire with special affection in their personal histories. In the last years of the 20th century it was decided that the Hospital must close. The University of Derby had just merged with High Peak College with premises at Harpur Hill above the town. We were looking to relocate to the town centre so that we could embed our vision of lifelong learning at the heart of the community. It was our good fortune to be able to acquire this magnificent building from the National Health Service. It is now our challenge to give it a new lease of life by developing a centre of excellence in learning which will serve the needs of the community, give an economic boost to the town, and address the broader needs of the hospitality and tourism industry across the County and beyond. Our dream is to become recognised as an international centre of excellence. We could have no finer premises in which to realise it.

UNIVERSITY
of DERBY COLLEGE
BUXTON

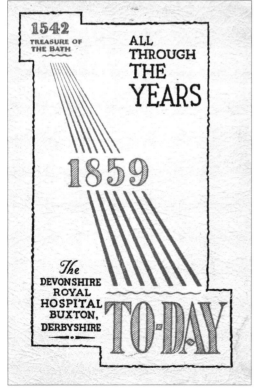

An Appeal

WE appeal to you with all the earnestness of which we are capable for your generous assistance in this great work.

Your cheque book is no doubt handy—please, therefore, do not put this appeal aside but post to us your assistance without delay, thus encouraging others by your example and us to further effort.

Gifts of £1,000 and upwards will be recorded in perpetuity by the naming of a bed.

Possibly you would also like to assist us annually.

Generous privileges are accorded to Annual Subscribers, and further information on this or any other point will be gladly supplied by the General Superintendent at the Hospital.

The cover and the Appeal from the 1939 Proposals for the Hospital.

INTRODUCTION

The inland resort of Buxton has some fine architecture, a perambulation in the town will reveal the 16th century Old Hall Hotel, a magnificent Georgian Crescent and other 18th century buildings in both the higher and lower town. All around you will see good quality Victorian buildings in both a public and private use.

The astute observer will also see many domes both large and small. The Opera House of 1903 has two and, alongside it, on the entrance to the Pavilion Gardens, are two glass domes. In the Pavilion Gardens is the large concert hall, known as the Octagon, for its octagonal domed roof. The original Peak Hydro on Terrace Road, now the Museum and Art Gallery, has one, and opposite, the Town Hall, though French Chateau in style, has a cupola in the centre of its roof. St John's Church, of 1811, has a small dome as part of its Italianate design.

The use of a dome in building design was taken up by the local architects in the 19th and 20th centuries and a number of large houses boast a dome, with examples in College Road, The Park and Burlington Road. But the largest and most prominent dome in town is that of the Devonshire Royal Hospital. It dominates the sky-line and it is difficult for us today to imagine how the town would look without this magnificent architectural feature.

What is it about a dome which attracts architect and lay person alike? The Millennium Dome at Greenwich may not have been considered an economic success but it was, nevertheless, a most outstanding piece of architecture. Why did Brunelleschi, in the 15th century, create a dome for the Cathedral at Florence, described by Leon Battista Alberti as

'...A structure so enormous, as high as the heavens,
big enough to cover all of Tuscany with its shadow...'

and why did Sir Christopher Wren incorporate a large dome into St Paul's Cathedral at the end of the 17th century after the great fire of London?

Perhaps in sacred buildings we may perceive a symbolic 'reaching to heaven' or provision of a safe and embracing shelter for all those who believe and worship God. Thus we see many large religious buildings incorporating a domed roof or featuring a dome as part of the construction; St Peter's Rome, many examples in Venice including the magnificent church of Della Salute, that of Saints Simeone and Guida and, of course, the Basilica of St Mark, which has no less than five domes to its roof.

In 19th century England the dome was to be more frequently designed into secular buildings and the designer of Buxton's hospital dome had many such buildings for comparison, the British Library Reading Room of 1854-57 by Sydney Smirke, the International Exhibition of 1862, designed by Captain Francis Fowke, which featured a 160 feet diameter glass dome at each end, and the Albert Hall of 1867-71, by Lieutenant-Colonal H.Y.D. Scott.

The dome construction was a bold statement of the architect's courage as well as of competence in design. But it was also used to make a public statement of the importance of the building it crowned, the basilica, the exhibition hall, the town hall, the public museum or reading room, these were all important representations. So it was at Buxton where Robert Rippon Duke, the architect personally involved in the work and management of the institution, undoubtedly wished to place that institution - the Devonshire Hospital - firmly on the map. This was a significant statement of the importance of the work of the hospital and the value of the Buxton thermal mineral water in healing the sick poor.

Duke's dome roof was large and ambitious; the central dome was surrounded by a smaller dome, or cupola, on each corner, and a further dome surmounting the clock tower. It reinforced Buxton's reputation throughout the country, but it was also symbolic of a safe and embracing shelter for the sick.

This book is about the activity which has gone on within the walls of the building and under that dome. It describes the work of a hospital spanning nearly 150 years and it traces the history of the charity which has supported that work, a charity which had its roots in the 16th century and which delivered medical relief to the sick poor from 1779 to the start of the National Health Service in 1948. The Devonshire Royal Hospital developed a fine reputation for the treatment of rheumatic and arthritic and associated disease, it helped to develop the reputation of Buxton as an inland medical resort, and it has treated many hundreds of thousands of patients in its lifetime. It has overcome many difficulties to maintain its medical service and reputation.

The Devonshire Royal Hospital, its magnificent dome construction, and its unique work, is at the heart of Buxton life. Now that its work as a hospital has ceased, a new lease of life is planned; John Carr's stables and Robert Rippon Duke's domed hospital is to become a university campus and to play its part in turning Buxton into a university town. It is timely to tell the full story of this historic building and the humanitarian work which it supported.

CHAPTER ONE
Objects of Charity - The Buxton Bath Charity

Before looking at the Devonshire Hospital as a building and a working hospital, it is necessary to go back through time to look at the origins of the Buxton Bath Charity. For it is true to say that without this charity there would have been no hospital, its existence and growth as a medical centre, right up to the 1948 National Health Act, has been dependent upon charity funding and the direction of its charity trustees. This is exemplified by successive annual reports which have always recounted the work of the Devonshire Hospital and Buxton Bath Charity. It is right, therefore, that this chapter should look at the history and growth of the Buxton Bath Charity.

Elizabethan Origins

The first mention of a charity is to be found in Dr John Jones' book *The Benefit of the Auncient Bathes of Buckstones*, published 1572, the earliest medical treatise on the Buxton waters. Jones was intent upon establishing the reputation of Buxton as a medical spa and he put forward a plan whereby the poor might be treated and a resident physician might be paid for. His idea, which he called 'The Treasury of the Bath,' was to levy a sliding scale of charges on visitors to the bath according to their status and ability to pay. Thus he proposed:

> '...I would have every yeoman to pay 1s. every Gentleman 3s. every Esquire 3s.4d. every Knight 6s. 8d. every Lord and Baron 10s. every Viscount 13s.4d. every Earl 20s. every Marquess 30s. every Duke £3.10s every Archbishop £5. every Bishop 40s. every Judge 20s. every Doctor and Serjeant at Law 10s. every Counsellor and Outter Barrister 6s.8d. every Minister 1s. every Duchess 40s. every Marchioness 20s. every Countess 13s.4d. every Baroness 10s. every Lady 6s.8d. every Gentlewoman 2s. and all for the Treasury of the Bath, to the use of the poor, that only for help do come hither, the one half, the other to the Physician for his Residence. If any think this magisterial imposing on Peoples Pockets, let them consider their Abilities, and the sick Poors necessities, and think whether they do not in idle Pastimes throw away in vain twice as much yearly...'[1]*

Dr Jones' promotion of Buxton was greatly helped by the visits of Mary Queen of Scots who came to take the waters on at least five occasions between 1573 and 1584. With her came important members of Queen Elizabeth's court including the 6th Earl of Shrewsbury, her gaoler, who built the Hall in 1572/3 (now the Old Hall Hotel); The Lord Treasurer, Lord Burghley; Secretary of State, Sir Thomas Smith; Lord Gilbert and Lady Mary Talbot; and, most influentially Robert Dudley, Earl of Leicester and favourite of Queen Elizabeth. Bess of Hardwick, wife of the Earl of Shrewsbury, used her undeniable business acumen to promote the use of the Hall and bath at a time when the secular holiday was beginning to emerge and resorting to spas was becoming fashionable.[2]

Buxton's chief rival, Bath in Somerset, was host to Queen Elizabeth in August 1574 where she held a privy council and stayed for five days during her progress in the south west. In the royal progress in the summer of 1576, the Earl of Leicester, receiving treatment for gout, was advised that, wherever he went, he must drink Buxton water for twenty consecutive days. Although Queen Elizabeth did not actually visit the spa, so full of praise was the Earl of Leicester for the Buxton water that, shortly after his return to court in July 1577, she asked for a tun of water to be sent to her in hogsheads, although he noted that she was not disposed to make any use of it.[3]

Despite this popularity, Dr Jones' recommendations were not acted upon and no charity emerged at this time, though the increasing numbers of poor people resorting to both Buxton and Bath did give rise to problems for the inhabitants. In 1572 an act was passed to deal with the large numbers of poor and diseased persons going to the baths. It was part of a wider measure dealing with the punishment of vagabonds and for relief of the poor and impotent. The section dealing with Buxton and Bath required that all diseased or impotent people living on alms should be licensed by two Justices of the Peace of their own county and that their own parish should be responsible for their maintenance before they set off to visit the bath. Furthermore, the licence was for a specified period of time beyond which they were not allowed to remain at the expense of either the town of Buxton or Bath but would be treated as vagabonds.

This act may have not been wholly effective for, in 1595 the inhabitants of the village of Fairfield, adjacent to the bath at Buxton, petitioned Queen Elizabeth for support in maintaining their own chapel and in their plea included the expense of upkeeping poor sick people who travelled to the baths at Buxton for treatment. The requirements of the 1572 act were repeated in a further act of 1597/98 with the additional clause that paupers at the bath should not beg, so perhaps the petition of the people of Fairfield had wider repercussions.[4] Some poor sick people were licensed to travel and were given help to visit the Buxton bath within the terms of the act. In 1609 the City of York allowed Anthony Cuthbert, a poor lame boy, 5 shillings to go to St Anne's Well at Buxton for the sake of his health. The accounts of Lady Arbella Stuart show that in 1609 she gave 13s. 4d. for the benefit of the poor at Buxton bath.[5]

Bathing Provision for the Poor

Unlike Bath there was no organised provision made for the poor in Buxton during the 17th century. In Bath there were two hospitals offering some limited places for the poor and one hospital which treated the leprous poor. In about 1609 Thomas Bellott endowed a charity which provided the land and building of Bellott's Hospital in Bell Tree Lane, and land elsewhere to provide an income. This was for the poor lame people who came to Bath on a magistrate's licence and it may be seen as an embryonic hospital since the services of a surgeon were provided, and free access to the hot springs for up to four weeks per patient. Subsequent endowments maintained the services of a visiting physician and the hospital, which was administered by the corporation, and could take up to sixteen patients at any one time.[6]

Buxton had no similar hospital but, at the very end of the century, some modest provision was made in the construction of an open bath for the poor. The tenant of the Hall, Cornelius White, who was an attorney of His Majesty's Court of Kings-Bench at Westminster, made a number of important improvements to the Hall and bath, which included repairs to the original bath and a new bath constructed for the poor and impotent. Cornelius White also had a sough laid which allowed both baths to be drained for cleaning, a tremendous step forward in hygiene. This 'poor bath' was built on land to the north of the inner or old bath and was walled round, but open to the elements; it was known as 'White's Bath'. The outer bath dimensions were 17 feet long by 10 foot 2 inches wide and it had a water depth of 5 feet 4 inches; it was fed from the overflow of the inner bath.[7] This provided Buxton with a facility for the poor but there is little evidence to suggest how and by whom

BUXTON BATH CHARITY

Instituted for the relief of POOR PERSONS from all parts of Great Britain and Ireland suffering from

RHEUMATISM and GOUT, SCIATICA, Pains, Weakness, or Contractions of Joints or Limbs, arising from these diseases, or from **SPRAINS, FRACTURES**, or other local injuries; **CHRONIC FORMS of PARALYSIS; DROPPED HANDS** and other poisonous effects of Lead, Mercury, or other Minerals; Spinal affections; Dyspeptic Complaints; Uterine obstructions, &c.

SUPPORTED BY VOLUNTARY CONTRIBUTIONS.

PATRONS.

The Duke of Devonshire, K.G.

The Duke of Norfolk, K.G.   The Duke of Rutland, K.G.

PRESIDENT.

Lord Viscount Combermere, G.C.B.

VICE-PRESIDENTS.

Sir Roderick Impey Murchison, F.R.S.

E. S. Chandos Pole, Esq., *Radbourn Hall.*

Edmund Denison, Esq., M.P., *Doncaster.*

William Evans, Esq., M.P., *Allestree Hall.*

Richard Bethell, Esq., *The Rise, Hull.*

Roger Hall, Esq., *Narrow Water, Ireland.*

Daniel Grant, Esq., *Manchester.*

Richard Fosbroke Buckley, Esq., *Chester.*

Edmund Buckley, Esq., *Manchester.*

TRUSTEES.

The Right Reverend Lord Bishop Spencer.

The Reverend R. P. Hull Brown.

Sydney Smithers, Esq.

Samuel Grimshawe, Esq.

W. H. Robertson, Esq., M.D.

Thomas Carstairs, Esq., M.D.

W. P. Shipton, Esq. M.R.C.S.

TREASURER----Sydney Smithers, Esq.

RULES.

A donation of £10 shall constitute a Subscriber for life, with power to send a Patient annually.

A Subscriber of One Guinea may recommend a Patient to the full benefit of the Charity who shall be entitled to receive Medical advice, Medicines, the use of the Baths, and to a Gratuity of Five Shillings weekly, for the period of three weeks.

A Subscriber of Half-a-Guinea may recommend a Patient, who shall be entitled to receive Medical advice, Medicines, the use of the Baths, and to a Gratuity of Half-a-Crown weekly, for the period of three weeks.

A Subscriber of Half-a-Crown, and under Half-a-Guinea, may recommend a Patient, who shall be entitled to receive Medical advice, Medicines, and the use of the Baths, without pecuniary assistance.

Any person in need of the use of the Charity Baths will be admitted thereto on producing a certificate from the Clergyman of his or her Parish, or from his or her Medical Attendant, of inability to pay for the same; subject to the sanction of one of the Medical Trustees of the Charity.

Boards of Guardians and Friendly Societies shall be allowed to send a Patient annually for every Guinea Subscribed.

By Order of the Trustees,
JAMES WARDLEY, Secretary.

BUXTON, May 1st, 1853.

JOHN C. BATES, Printer, Bookseller, and Stationer, 6, Hall Bank, Buxton.

Poster advertising the work of the Buxton Bath Charity issued in 1853 and printed by the local firm of John Cumming Bates. Note the list of very aristocratic and distinguished patrons.

the poor were treated in the early part of the 18th century. Daniel Defoe, visiting in 1727, described only one bath, although Dr Short, writing in 1734, described 'White's Bath' being used as a ladies' bath. Dr Hunter, in his treatise on Buxton published in 1768, does not mention the poor bath, but John Whittaker's *History of Manchester,* published in 1771, mentions the:

> '...*springs which now feed the great bagnio immediately above, and the overflowings of which supply the lesser bagnio for the poor below...*'[8]

Meanwhile the wealthy residents of Bath had taken steps to cope with beggars coming to the baths in growing numbers after the act of 1572 had lapsed in 1714. Between 1738 and 1742 the Bath General Hospital (now the Royal National Hospital for Rheumatic Diseases) was built to take patients from all parts of the country. Admission was tightly controlled by the Hospital Bill of 1738 and only those sponsored by a responsible person as worthy of charity were accepted as patients. This hospital, as a significant philanthropic institution, enhanced the reputation of the spa nationally and gave doctors the opportunity to advance their professional stature and career. The same would be true of Buxton but not for another 120 years.[9]

The Earliest Operation of the Charity

Buxton did however have a resident doctor in Samuel Buxton, who was born in or near the town in 1747 and remained in Buxton until his death in 1826, becoming apothecary in 1769 and surgeon in 1779 and, at some point, acquiring the degree of Doctor of Medicine. It is likely that Dr Buxton was an instigator of the charity which was formed in 1779 with the aim of improving the poor bath and extending its use, since there is evidence to suggest that the bath had not been well maintained.[10] The writer, William Bray, described the early operation of the charity as follows:

> '...*whoever happens to be at the head of the table, collects one shilling from every new comer on his first appearance, for the benefit of the poor; the same is done at the other houses, and the whole amounts to a handsome sum in the season...*' [11]

The stewards of the hotels and lodging houses, who initially ran the charity, collected and recorded all contributions before paying them over to Samuel Buxton, the treasurer. By these means it was possible to support a number of poor people taking treatment and to provide a weekly allowance for their lodgings, as described by a local man William Bott in 1795:

> '...*The poor at their bath are not only exempted from all charge, but also meet with great assistance and support from the charitable contributions of the company who resort to Buxton, as it is customary for every new comer, if he stays more than one day, to give one shilling for their use, which is collected and taken care of by the steward of the house in which he happens to lodge: and the sum raised in this way in the course of the season, has some years past been very considerable. The common weekly allowance to the poor is six shillings, and should any of them be more weak and necessitous then it is usual to add something more...* '[12]

The charity was put on a formal footing in 1785, when the rules were revised and set out in a resolution of the stewards of the hotels and lodging houses on behalf of the contributors. These rules covered the auditing of accounts and specified those who could take advantage of the charity. No person residing in Buxton, Fairfield, or within seven miles of the baths, could be admitted and no one could come during the months of November to April. All prospective patients had to be recommended by a person of repute, or a churchwarden or overseer of the poor in the case of a pauper, and the written application was required to contain a certificate from a physician or apothecary confirming that the case was suitable for treatment by Buxton waters. The cost of travel to and from Buxton had to be paid by those recommending, who were also required to provide the cost of burial should the patient die at or within seven miles of the town. A maximum of 16 patients were taken and the days and times when they could be admitted were set out. Patients were to be admitted for a maximum period of five weeks, and supplied with board, lodging and medicines up to six shillings per week though the amount and cost of stay could be varied on the recommendation of the physician and at the treasurer's discretion. No patient was allowed to beg during their time at Buxton and any swearing, drunkenness or gross misbehaviour would result in the patient being discharged from the charity. These rules, though extended and further refined, formed the basis of the charity throughout its 170 years of existence.[13]

By 1811 the bath charity, described as the 'Charitable Institution', was managed by a committee which included two of the most influential people in town, Phillip Heacock, agent to the Devonshire Buxton Estate, and George Goodwin, the banker. Mr Peter Flint, a dentist and apothecary, was the secretary, and he later became senior surgeon and consulting apothecary. The charity expanded quite quickly, in 1811 there were 150 patients treated, the annual report of 1822 showed 796 patients and up to the mid-century the number of patients ranged between 800 and 1200 in the year, with a high in 1842 of 1477. Patients came from throughout the country, although a predominance were from the cotton districts of Lancashire and Cheshire in occupations such as cotton operatives, weavers, carders and machinists; other occupations ranged from domestic servants to colliers and miners and large numbers of labourers. Although the Buxton waters were valued for the treatment of rheumatic disease and gout, a wide range of conditions were presented by charity patients, including forms of paralysis, stroke, rheumatic fever and glandular swellings, as well as neuralgia, sciatica and various forms of rheumatism.[14]

Sir Charles Scudamore MD, as honorary physician of the charity, referred to the annual report of 1830 and the remarks of the chairman for the year, Charles C. Western MP., later Lord Western. He pointed out that Buxton is within a short distance of the manufacturing towns of Leeds, Manchester, Sheffield, Birmingham, Macclesfield and Stockport, and observed that many workers, broken down by the confinement and and unhealthy nature of their employments, arrive in Buxton as miserable spectacles of accumulated disease, but go home after treatment with their health and strength restored. He also observed that the medicinal qualities of the water were valuable, not only for cases of rheumatism and gout but in almost all cases of...

' ...*debilitated and broken-down constitutions, the effects of acute or chronic disease, climate or intemperance, as well as the unhealthy occupation of the workmen in manufacturing towns, the most beneficial results are experienced from the use of the baths and the waters taken internally. The powers of the digestive organs are wonderfully restored: the skin being brought into a more healthy state by the bath, aids the relief given to the stomach by the water which is drunk, and thus a healthy action of the whole system is brought about, the patient is restored to his former vigour, and a condition of permanent health...* [15]

Such observations by influential and eminent chairmen did much to develop the reputation of the Buxton Bath Charity.

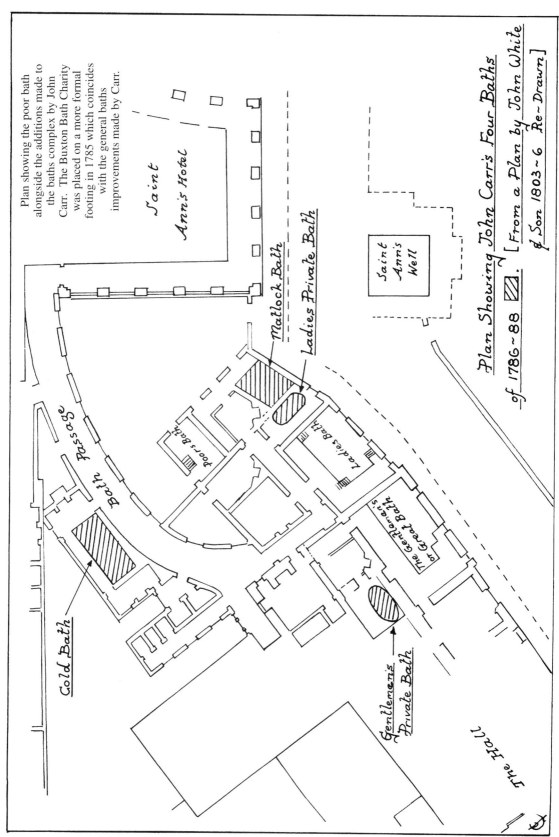

Plan showing the poor bath alongside the additions made to the baths complex by John Carr. The Buxton Bath Charity was placed on a more formal footing in 1785 which coincides with the general baths improvements made by Carr.

Saint Ann's Hotel

Saint Ann's Well

Matlock Bath

Ladies Private Bath

Bath Passage

Poor's Bath

Ladies Bath

Cold Bath

The Gentlemen's or The Great Bath

Gentleman's Private Bath

The Hall

Plan Showing John Carr's Four Baths of 1786~88 ▨. [From a Plan by John White & Son 1803~6 Re~Drawn]

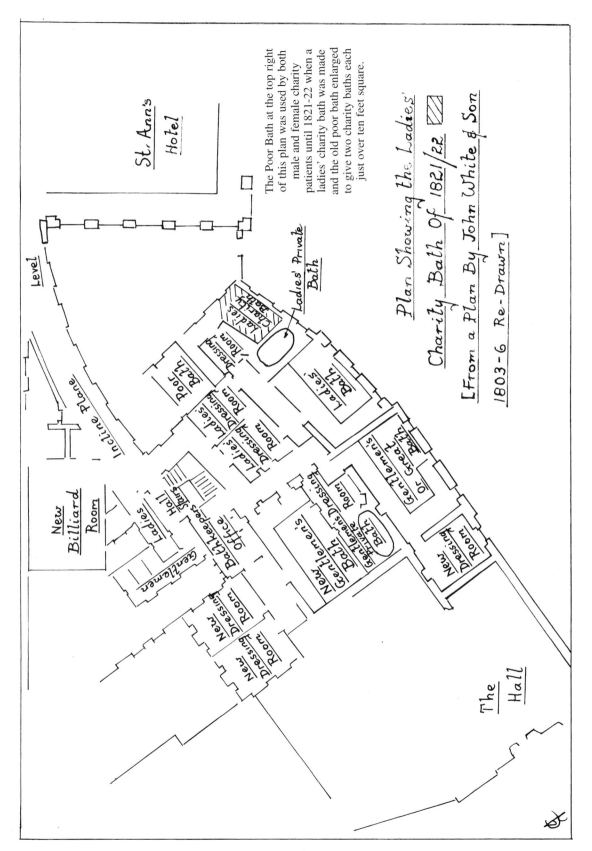

St. Ann's Hotel

The Poor Bath at the top right of this plan was used by both male and female charity patients until 1821-22 when a ladies' charity bath was made and the old poor bath enlarged to give two charity baths each just over ten feet square.

Level

New Billiard Room

Incline Plane

Ladies

Ladies' Dressing Room

Poor Bath

Dressing Room

Ladies' Charity Bath

Ladies' Private Bath

Ladies Bath

Gentlemen

Backkeepers Office

Hall Stairs

New Dressing Room

New Dressing Room

Gentlemen's Dressing Room

Gentlemen's Bath

Gentlemen's Private Bath

Gentlemen's Great or Bath

New Dressing Room

The Hall

Plan Showing the Ladies'
Charity Bath of 1821/22 ▨
[From a Plan By John White & Son]
1803-6 Re-Drawn

Providing for Patients

The Revd. R. Ward, writing in 1827, offers a religious perspective and seeks to invite his reader to be compassionate to the poor by supporting the charity. He presents his reader with a short homily on why it is a salutary experience to come to Buxton to see, and perhaps help, those less fortunate in health than oneself and he offers an apposite piece of verse:

O! pause awhile, whoe're thou art
That drink this healing stream;
If e'er compassion in thy heart
Diffus'd its heavenly beam;

Think on the wretch, whose distant lot
This friendly aid denies
Think how, in some poor lonely cot,
He unregarded lies.

Hither the helpless stranger bring,
Relieve his heartfelt woe,
And let thy bounty, like this spring,
In genial currents flow.

So may thy years from grief and pain,
And pining want be free:
And though from heav'n that mercy gain,
The poor receive from thee... [16]

His sentiment was fully supported by members of his profession by the annual sermons preached at St John's and other Buxton churches, right throughout the 19th century, to raise funds for the charity. A more prosaic description of life as a charitable patient was given by 'J.E.' of Todmorden, who composed a 22 verse poem on his experiences; here is just a flavour of his doggerel:

The doctors are Bennet, Turner, and Dickson,
And Sykes the dispenser who attends to prescriptions;
They give us medicine according to our disorder,
And baths by degrees in regular order.

There are hot baths at one hundred, ninety five, and at ninety,
Then get eighty six you approach Natural quietly;
Arriving at this you get strength very fast.
And rejoice at the remedy you're finding at last... [17]

Until about 1840 the patients were seen by the doctor in a somewhat cold and bare room known as the Bath Yard, at the back of the Old Hall Hotel. In this room, which also housed the one bath-chair owned by the charity, it is recorded that Sir Charles Scudamore MD used a drum-head as a table in his consultations with patients. By 1843, however, a waiting and consulting room at the bottom of Terrace Road (also known as Yeoman's Lane) was rented from the Devonshire Estate; the secretary, Mr Mugliston's house was nearby.[18] Patients would walk from their lodgings to the consulting room and to the charity baths, situated in the Crescent, for treatment. The single 'poors bath' was of gritstone, now measuring eight feet square, and was supplied by water overflow from the Great Bath. It remained the only such bath and was used by both male and female charity patients

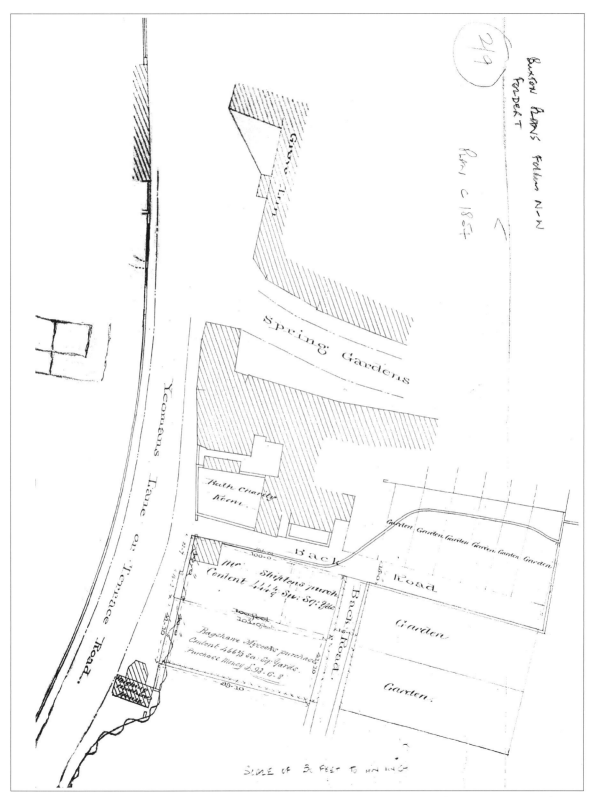

By 1843 a proper waiting and consulting room was provided for charity patients. This was at the bottom of Terrace Road (also known as Yeoman's Lane) and was rented from the Devonshire Estate.

until 1821-22 when a ladies' charity bath was made and the old charity bath enlarged to give two baths each just over ten feet square. This provision remained until the baths were entirely rebuilt by Henry Currey in 1851-54, from which time separate charity baths for men and women were provided in both the Natural and Hot Baths buildings. These baths offered a much improved facility and were described by Dr W.H. Robertson as follows:

' ...The baths of the water at the natural temperature provided for the use of the patients of the Buxton Bath Charity, are equal in every essential particular to those [for the paying patients]. The Men's Charity Bath is contained in an apartment which is twenty-six feet six inches long and twenty feet wide; the bath itself being twenty feet long and fifteen feet wide. There are dressing boxes and every needful comfort, and a douche closet for the separate application of the douche without immersion. The Women's Charity Bath apartment is thirty feet long and twenty feet wide; the bath being twenty feet long and fifteen feet wide. There are dressing boxes, douche closet &c. Both these baths are lighted, warmed, ventilated, and supplied in every particular, as satisfactorily as the other baths...[19]

Engraving of the front of the Hot Baths of 1854 (centre) taken from an album issued by
the publisher, J.C.Bates, in about 1865.

He also described the Charity Hot Baths:

' ...The [Charity] baths are approached by an entrance on the north of the building. There are separate bath-rooms for men and for women, each containing two baths, with dressing-closets, douche-closet &c., and entered from a comfortable waiting room... [20]

This was a significant step forward in the quality of charity bath provision and a measure of the importance with which the charity and its honorary medical advisers were viewed. It is notable, however, that charity patients were segregated from paying patients having, at the rear of each baths, their own separate entrance.

Engraving of the front of the Natural Baths of 1854 (extreme right) taken from an album issued by the publisher J.C.Bates in about 1865

The St Anne's Well Women, appointed annually at the Vestry meeting, served the natural mineral water at the drinking well. They were required as part of their duties to help the poor women in the bath and clean drying mats, bathing gowns, towels and the bath. It is not known who provided similar service in the mens' bath, but cleanliness may have been somewhat lacking since a Quaker visitor, one Thomas Shillitoe, was so concerned after visiting the men bathing that he walked to Chatsworth to complain to the Duke of Devonshire about the conditions. Evidently the Buxton Devonshire Estate Agent, Phillip Heacock, was not pleased at Shillitoe appealing directly to the duke, and said so, but conditions at both Charity Baths did improve thereafter. In 1840 the trustees of the charity decided to appoint their own female bath attendant.

Rules of the Charity

As the charity progressed the rules were modified from time to time. By January 1823 patients received 5 shillings per week for three weeks and this was the case up to 1840 when it was resolved that a donation of £10 would give life membership for a subscriber and power to send one patient annually. In 1854 it was agreed that a patient's stay could be extended to four weeks if needed and patient benefits became dependent upon the size of donation from their sponsor. A one guinea subscriber could nominate a patient to receive 5s. per week for 3 weeks plus treatment. A half guinea subscriber patient received 2s 6d. per week and treatment for three weeks, and a subscriber of less than half guinea, but more than 2s.6d., could nominate a patient to receive treatment only. Not all patients, however, needed financial assistance and a number came each year to receive the diagnosis and treatment only, on a free basis. It will be realised that the sum of 5s., even in the mid 19th century, was a small amount to provide weekly accommodation, and patients were placed in very modest lodgings, often some distance from the lower town and the baths. Patients would have to walk to the baths and back to lodgings after treatment, which could not have helped their recovery, and this was one of the arguments put forward by the medical doctors in their attempt to secure a hospital.

Honorary Doctors

The role of the honorary physician or surgeon to the Buxton Bath Charity was very significant. It was through the influence of the medical officers that the charity was able to develop as an important asset to the town, but at the same time it enhanced the doctor's reputation. Doctors would use the statistics obtained from patients of the charity to support their reputation and that of the Buxton water. It was the practice to set out a record each year of the effect of treatment on patients. So, for example, in 1831, 724 were described as 'cured or much relieved', 52 as 'relieved' and 27 as 'no better'. By 1854 the descriptive term 'relieved' had changed to 'somewhat relieved' and, during the early life of the Devonshire Hospital, the term 'cured' was dropped, performance in 1878 being described as 1459 'relieved' and 55 'no better'.

From its inception to the early part of the 20th century, no less than 25 doctors were honorary medical officers of the charity, and they included all the best known practitioners in the town. The names of R.O.G. Bennet, Thomas Carstairs, T.J. Page, John Armitage Pearson and the Shiptons, father and sons were, amongst others, to become synonymous with the reputation of Buxton as a medical resort and the Buxton Bath Charity as a national medical resource. The most important of these doctors was, however, William Henry Robertson (1810-1897), who began his association with the charity as honorary physician in 1837. Dr Robertson was a prime mover in obtaining a hospital for the Buxton Bath Charity and in developing the medical services, as will be seen in later chapters.

Charity patients entered the Natural Baths in the Crescent by a rear entrance off the Square. It is the door to the right of the round arch in the background of the picture and it led down a slope to a further door into the baths. After 1876 this was the entrance to the 'new' Charity Bath situated under the roadway between the Old Hall Hotel and the Square.

The Quest for a Hospital

From quite early the annual meeting of the charity was chaired by a person of standing, thus in 1833 the Duke of Northumberland was in the chair, and in 1854, the noted author Sir Edward Bulwer Lytton, Bart., MP was chairman, and Viscount Combermere was president of the charity. [21] As in some previous years, the charity had advertised at 100 railway stations (even though Buxton had yet to obtain a railway connection) and the local publisher, J.C. Bates, produced a large, linen backed, poster describing the work of the charity.

Having suffered from a poor income in the 1840s, the charity was, in the early 1850s, financially well off, and it was in 1854 that the question of accommodation was raised. The honorary medical staff were strongly in favour of establishing a charity hospital because this would overcome the difficulties associated with patients being accommodated in lodging houses, and it would place Buxton on a par with Bath, where, as we have noted earlier, a General Hospital had been in existence for nearly 120 years; and also Harrogate, which obtained its charity 'Bath Hospital' in 1825. [22] The trustees wanted to establish a hospital close to the baths using some of their accrued funds and by raising further finance. The estimated cost of the project was put at £2,500 and an appeal was launched with a donation of £100 from the sixth Duke of Devonshire (1790-1858). The duke also offered a plot of land for the building at a convenient site.

By December 1855, the accumulated funds had reached £1,800 and it was decided to hold a grand bazaar in August 1856, in the ballroom of the Crescent Hotel, to make up the shortfall. This bazaar was held under the patronage of families of the nobility and aristocracy who were trustees or supporters of the charity. These included the Duchess of Norfolk, the Duchess of Sutherland, the Viscountess Combermere, Lady Waterpark, Lady Louisa Cavendish and Mrs Legh of Lyme Hall. Amongst the organisations providing a stall was the newly formed Buxton, Fairfield and Burbage Mechanics and Literary Institute. In 1857, with the proceeds from the successful bazaar of £844, and generous donations, the charity already held £3300 towards realising its ambition.

Plans were drawn up by Henry Currey, architect to the Duke of Devonshire, for a building to accommodate 84 patients to be sited on land in Sylvan Park. Sydney Smithers, the duke's Buxton agent, died in July 1856 and was replaced by Mr E. Woollett Wilmot, who became a trustee of the hospital and soon took up the question of the building. After making himself acquainted with the details, he concluded that the site chosen was not suitable because it had a northern aspect with a hill at the rear which would exclude sunlight, and at the front the River Wye would make it damp and cold. Wilmot was treasurer of the charity and in the 1857 accounts, he also informed subscribers that, taking into account furnishing, the total cost of the proposed accommodation was £6000, a figure which could not be reduced despite careful re-calculations. [23]

This site was, therefore turned down and the design shelved. However an engineer called Alfred Wilkins was in town taking the water treatment with some success and, being a talented model maker, he decided, perhaps in appreciation for the treatment he received, to make a scale model of the proposed building and present it to the Duke of Devonshire. He borrowed the plans of the 'Convalescent Home' and proceeded to build the model to such a degree of perfection that the individual roof slates were visible and real glass was put in the windows. Unfortunately the duke died before the model was completed but the model was later acquired from Wilkins' son Fred, by local architect and charity trustee, Robert Rippon Duke, who presented it to the hospital in 1900, the

Henry Currey, Arch.t

Day & Son, Lith.rs to The Queen

BUXTON BATH CHARITY.
VIEW OF PROPOSED LODGING HOUSE.

A Bazaar and Fancy Fair.

Will be held in the Great Ball Room at Buxton in the month of August 1856, in aid of the Fund for providing additional and more convenient lodging for the Poor resorting to Buxton for the benefit of the Baths and Waters.

PATRONESSES.

The Duchess of Norfolk, Glossop Hall, Derbyshire.

The Duchess of Sutherland, Trentham, Staffordshire.

The Viscountess Combermere, Combermere Abbey, Cheshire.

Lady Waterpark, Doveridge Hall, Derby.

Lady Louisa Cavendish, Ashford Hall, Bakewell.

Lady Crewe, Calke Abbey, Derby.

M.rs Thornhill, Stanton Hall, Bakewell.

M.rs Legh, Lyme Hall, Cheshire.

The distance from the Baths at which many of the Charity Patients are at present compelled to lodge, renders it both difficult and in many cases when crippled or infirm, very distressing to them to reach the Baths with that regularity which is so essential to insure to them the greatest possible amount of good to be derived from the Waters.

In order to obviate this disadvantage, and at the same time to enlarge the

Henry Currey's proposed accommodation for charity patients is shown on this poster for a bazaar to raise funds. This accommodation, planned for 84 patients to be sited on land in Sylvan Park, was not built. The design was subsequently used to provide the Wye House Private Asylum on Corbar Hill in 1859-60 which was run for many years by the Dickson family.

Penzance,
25ᵗʰ October 1900.

To
Robert R. Duke Esqⁱ
Park House, Buxton

"History of the Model."

The model now in your posession was given to me by my father, but owing to circumstances I have not sufficient room to do such a beautiful piece of work justice — and having learned that you remember the model, and that you are one of the oldest trustees connected with the affair, I was very pleased to send it you for acceptance — and I feel proud to know that you have given it such a kindly greeting — and that it has found a grand resting place in memory of my father —

An engineer and talented model-maker, Alfred Wilkins made a scale model of Henry Currey's proposed 'Convalescent Home'. This model was given by Wilkins' son, Fred, to local architect and charity trustee, Robert Rippon Duke who presented it to the hospital. Here is part of Fred Wilkin's letter to R.R. Duke.

year he was chairman of the trustees. [24]

The Devonshire Buxton Agent, Edward Woollett Wilmot, had other ideas for a charity hospital. Despite opposition from such notables as Sir Joseph Paxton, Bishop Spencer, and some of the medical staff, Wilmot ultimately persuaded the duke to allow a considerable part of the Great Stables to be converted into a hospital providing 110 beds and land adjoining for garden ground. The project was estimated to cost £4000 and the building would be conveyed under a nominal Chief Ground Rent.

The Great Stables, designed by John Carr of York, and built 1785-89, offered a most impressive hospital building for the Buxton Bath Charity and work began under the architect Henry Currey, with a new road being put in from the Quadrant in June 1857. As part of his proposals, E.W. Wilmot determined that the new accommodation (he made no mention of hospital but called it 'Lodging Houses for the Buxton Bath Charity') would be vested in and managed by a committee composed of 15 or 20 trustees, to be chosen from the subscribers, rather than the management board of seven local trustees as previously. After almost 80 years of charitable work, the Buxton Bath Charity, now reformed and strengthened under a new trust deed, was to begin a new chapter which would see it forge a national reputation as The Devonshire Hospital and Buxton Bath Charity.

In the 1914 Guide to the Devonshire Hospital a strong comparison was made between Carr's stables and the Palace of the Christian Kings in Granada, as depicted in 1707 (above).
The suggestion was that Carr's inspiration was from this building, and the illustration is indeed very much as the stables would have appeared before conversion to the hospital.

CHAPTER TWO
The Devonshire Hospital is born

Henry Currey (1820-1900) was faced with a most unusual conversion. Instead of supervising the building of a new hospital of his own design he was to partly convert a set of stables into hospital accommodation, leaving the remainder for their original use. But these were no ordinary stables. Built 1785-89 and designed by John Carr, one of the most competent and successful Georgian architects, who practised in Yorkshire and the north of England for more than half a century,[25] the stables were described as

'...the finest in Europe...' [26]

'...a fine range of buildings [whose] style of architecture happily corresponds with the grandeur of the [Crescent]...' [27]

The Great Stables are positioned on rising ground to the north west of the town centre and in a commanding position. The design is an irregular octagon with a circular Doric colonnade or 'circus' inside to provide a covered riding house.[28] Designed to stable 120 horses around the 180 foot diameter circle, the stables provided quarters for servants and ostlers on the first floor. *Pigot's Directory of Derbyshire* 1835 describes:

'...a riding house where the company take exercise on horseback when the weather renders shelter necessary...' [29]

A description repeated by Bagshaw in 1846, who also notes that the stables provide:

'...ample room for an immense number of horses and carriages...' [30]

- and the stables also housed the necessary services of a blacksmith. However, by 1857, demand at the stables had reduced and some parts of the building were rented by building, joinery and cabinet making businesses; the well known livery stable business of Samuel Fidler also offered horses and carts from the Great Stables. [31] This, then, was the challenge facing Henry Currey.

Work on the project began in 1858, overseen by Currey's Clerk of Works, William Robinson, and there is some evidence to suggest that the local building partnership of Samuel Turner and Robert Rippon Duke were employed as the main contractors.[32] The completed hospital conversion provided the much needed patient accommodation but was a far from satisfactory arrangement in terms of hygiene. The stables occupied one third of the building to the east and north sides and the patients were housed in the remaining two-thirds on the south and west. [33] The converted building opened in 1859 with accommodation for 65 male and 45 female patients, together with accident beds and staff quarters. [34]

The new part-hospital, part-stables incorporated a change in the main entrance which had formerly fronted onto Manchester Road. This was closed off to provide a dining hall across three bays of the elevation and a new entrance was provided on the south front with curved steps leading up. Separate entrances for the male and female sides of the building were opened on the Manchester Road facade and a passage was created against the outer encircling wall, giving access to a series of wards partitioned off, which had windows looking into the central colonnade. Beyond this the

Rare shot of the hospital from Corbar Hill c.1877, before the addition of the great dome which clearly shows the circular open area in the middle of the building.

The new entrance on the south front of the hospital after the 1859 conversions.

circular colonnade still provided a covered walkway, although, despite the suggestion on the plan of paths and planted borders, it is not clear that the patients had access to the central area. Indeed, it may have continued to be used to exercise horses for it was not until the R.R. Duke conversion 20 years later that the circular ride was incorporated into a hospital corridor.

On the ground floor each of the two corners fronting onto Manchester Road were used as day rooms, that to the north for men, and to the south for women. Henry Currey's plans show a first floor laid out entirely in hospital wards, except for rooms for the Master and Matron over the south front. These rooms could be reached by a separate staircase in the entrance hall. The conversion was carried out with good quality local materials where available, fresh lime ash from Grin Lime Kilns, stone from Henry Vicker's Nithen End quarry, and best stock bricks. The staircases were from clean

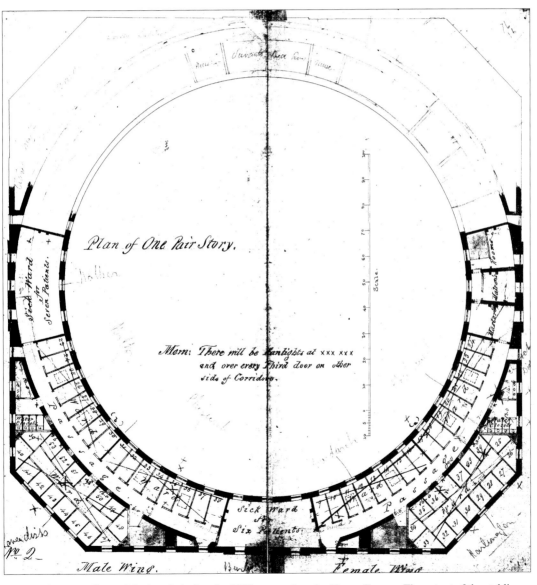

Plan of the upper floor of the hospital after the 1859 conversions by Henry Currey. The extent of the stabling given over to hospital use can be clearly seen. The upper floor was given to ward use, except for the master and matron accommodation.

yellow deal and had moulded handrails; ablution areas included good quality hand basins, and 'Jennings Imperishable Earthenware' water closets were fitted. The glazing specified best 'Newcastle Crown' glass.

Currey paid particular attention to heating and ventilation using two wrought iron boilers to warm the building and, although some of the fireplaces were rebuilt, the architect did not want these to take the place of the heating apparatus. The heating was through warming chambers, and ventilation was achieved through chambers connecting to large square louvred turrets on the roof . Although meals were to be of a 'plain kind' the specification included cooking stoves with rotating ovens and top ovens for pastry. A slightly later addition was the provision for the hospital to be lit by gas. [35] Later plans show the south eastern corner of the ground floor, adjoining the stabling, in use as a board room, doctors' room, dispensary and waiting room.[36]

Despite this progress, within a short time the charity trustees were applying pressure on the Duke of Devonshire, through his Buxton agent George Drewry, to relinquish the rest of the building so that the whole could be used as a hospital. A deputation of the hospital trustees met Drewry in January 1865 with this in mind, but were firmly rebuffed by the agent, who explained that it had not been envisaged by the estate office that the whole of the building should ever be used for this purpose. A note in a record of informal discussions held by the Buxton Estate Office, reveals Drewry's private irritation at this approach;

> '...Some of them [the trustees] appear to think that the whole of the building can be given up and used as a hospital when required. I wrote to Mr Currey [of Currey & Co.] to ask him what the late duke's intentions were respecting it. His answer was that nothing of the sort was ever intended or thought of...' [37]

Dr Robertson, as trustee and Hon. Physician at the hospital, continued to press for the rest of the building and, perhaps as a concessionary gesture, the duke offered the land in front of the hospital to the trustees of the charity in May 1865. The offer was duly accepted and the local builder/architect, Robert Rippon Duke, was commissioned to lay out the land. Part of this land was subsequently allotted to the Buxton Hotel Company who were building a new hotel (the Palace Hotel) on the land immediately to the east of the stables. The hotel project required the building of a new approach road which was also designed by Duke and could be used by both the hospital and the Hotel. This became the Devonshire Road which opened up Devonshire Park for building. Duke employed the head gardener of the Pavilion Gardens, Adam Hogg to design and lay out the paths, borders and plantings.

In 1868, the Duke of Devonshire formally conveyed some of the land and buildings to the trustees, consisting of the hospital, the pleasure grounds and land on the north, west and south sides, for a nominal rent of 5s. per annum. The rest of the building and land used as stabling, which was to the north and east of the site, was not transferred until 1878.[38]

Charity Baths

A series of drawings by Robert Rippon Duke, dated 1872, suggest that, should they eventually acquire the complete building, it was the intention of the hospital trustees to provide bathing facilities for its patients within the building. This would avoid the inconvenience of transporting the often elderly and infirm from the hospital to the charity baths which were situated in the hot and natural wings of the existing baths at either end of the Crescent.

The drawings show an octagonal bathhouse complex situated in the centre of the open rotunda of the Great Stables building. The level of detail on the drawings is insufficient to determine whether the structure was intended to be iron framed but similarities between it and the slightly later Concert Hall (also designed by Duke and built 1876) could suggest that this was the intention. [39] Later plans of 1875, also submitted by Duke, proposing the sinking of a 18,000 gallon tank some 60 feet below the level of the hospital, to be fed by water gravitationally from the Natural Baths then pumped vertically into baths at the hospital, were not considered practicable by the duke's agent. They also failed to meet the approval of Dr Robertson, Senior Physician at the hospital, who was strongly of the belief that the medical properties of the waters were adversely affected by the distance of the water supply from the spring source. The estimated cost of Duke's scheme,of between £5,000 and £10,000, was not considered to be affordable and the project did not proceed. [40]

However, separate baths for the exclusive use of the hospital charity patients were eventually supplied, by the provision of purpose built baths on land a little distance from the main baths buildings. Both were designed by Robert Rippon Duke and opened in 1876. The Natural temperature bath replaced the separate male and female baths in the main building and was ingeniously created underground behind the Old Hall Hotel. The entrance to this bath used the entrance of the Old Natural Charity Baths which was hidden out of sight of the paying bathers entering the building from the front. The bath was lined with white glazed bricks and the remains can still be seen today, though now minus a roof. It is often referred to as the 'Paupers' Bath', a not strictly accurate term as will be seen from this history. The new Charity Hot Baths were built on George Street, and contained separate male and female baths and changing facilities. The building is occupied today by an architectural practice on the left facing, and a bakery to the right. Large underground water storage tanks still remain under parts of the building. An extension was made at the eastern end in 1893 by the Devonshire Buxton Estate, to provide a laundry.

Acquisition of the Rest of the Building

The chairman of the trustees, Dr W H Robertson, was tenacious in seeking his goal of obtaining the whole of the building. As early as 1867 he was confident enough that the duke was about to relinquish the rest of the building to announce that he imminently expected to lay before the trustees the legal conveyance of the building and land. [41] This was, however, the indenture (or conveyance) relating to the 1858 conversion which was drawn up in June 1868. The duke's solicitor, William Currey, tempered their enthusiasm for obtaining the whole of the site with the legal nicety that a conveyance could not take place due to technical difficulties with the 'statute of Mortmain'.[42]

Another attempt was made in 1870 when the trustees attempted to woo the duke into handing over the rest of the building and in return the trustees would spend £2000 of hospital funds on the building of new stabling to replace those taken over for the purposes of the hospital. They suggested that land near the railway stations would be suitable for the replacement stables and that they were prepared to take on the expenditure necessary to convert the building should he agree to these arrangements. They were of the impression that the project could be completed by 1872. The duke was not persuaded and asked the trustees, through his agent, to rule out any further progress on the issue for the foreseeable future. [43]

Dr Robertson felt that the charity's own funds would be sufficient to incorporate the rest of the building into the hospital but in reality it soon became obvious that the cost of the conversion

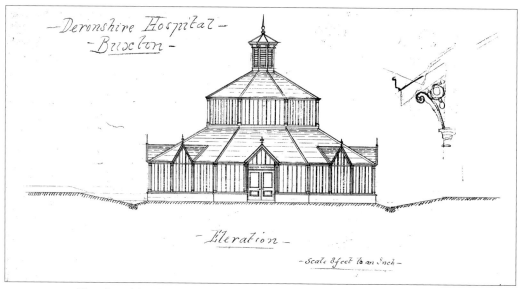

Elevation of the planned octagonal hospital baths in the centre of the hospital.
The detail suggests that this would have been an iron and glass pavilion of a similar style
to R.R. Duke's large concert hall of 1875 in the Pavilion Gardens.

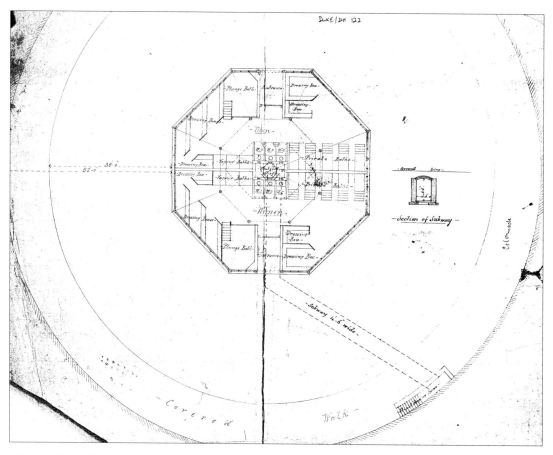

Robert Rippon Duke's plans of 1872 for baths in the centre of the open circular area in the middle of the hospital.
They were to be entered through a subway across the central area.

would be far and away above anything their existing funds could finance. During the negotiations leading up to the building of the new Charity Baths, contact had been made with the trustees of the Southport Convalescent and Sea Bathing Infirmary. The Southport organisation had recently been awarded a sizeable grant from the Cotton Famine Fund Committee to build the Southport Convalescent Home and the Southport Children's Sanatorium[44] and they felt that the Buxton Charity could also benefit by applying for a grant towards the building of the new Charity Baths and the cost of converting the remainder of the building, should they be successful in its acquisition from the Devonshire Estate.

1876 Charity Hot Baths building on George Street. Although not sporting its original roof, the elevations remain virtually unchanged. The building contained separate baths and changing facilities for both sexes.

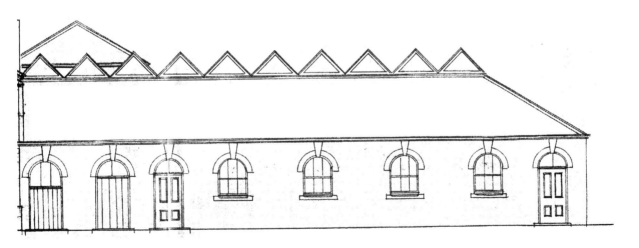

Architect's plan of the George Street baths, note the original ridge and furrow roofing designed to cope with the steam from the baths.

1876 Charity Natural Baths. This bath still exists underground behind the Old Hall hotel but is boarded up to prevent vandalism and no longer has a roof.

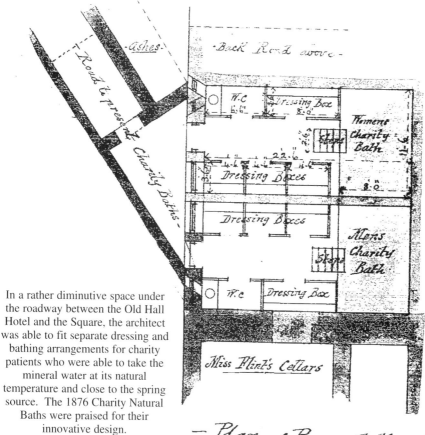

In a rather diminutive space under the roadway between the Old Hall Hotel and the Square, the architect was able to fit separate dressing and bathing arrangements for charity patients who were able to take the mineral water at its natural temperature and close to the spring source. The 1876 Charity Natural Baths were praised for their innovative design.

— Plan of Proposed New Charity Baths —

The Cotton District Convalescent Fund

The American Civil War, of 1861-65, badly disrupted the supply of raw cotton to Britain and consequently curtailed the employment of the cotton workers, centred predominantly in Lancashire. A famine resulted, particularly severe in the winter of 1862, which not only affected the cotton workers but also clerks, shopkeepers, warehouse men, tradesman and many others who relied on the cotton trade in the local economy. Cotton dominated Lancashire during this period; the census of 1861 shows that 384,000 people were employed in the industry. If the associated and ancillary workers are to be included the figure is increased to nearer one million. Furthermore if we assume that there were three dependents to each employee, the figure of four million people totally dependent on cotton gives an idea of the scale of the disaster. In 1862 the Lord Derby's Central (Executive) Relief Fund was set up to raise funds for the relief of the starving. Also known as the Fund for the Relief of Distress in the Manufacturing Districts, the Central Relief Fund and the Cotton Districts Relief Fund, a civil servant, Sir James Kay-Shuttleworth, was appointed as its secretary.

After the famine was over the fund had accumulated a large amount of money and it was decided that it could be put to other uses. Sir James Kay-Shuttleworth renamed the organisation The Cotton District Convalescent Fund (CDCF) and set about distributing the remaining funds to needy causes. The first beneficiary of the fund was Southport as mentioned earlier and it was by their recommendation that the Buxton trustees applied to the fund to help finance the hospital conversions. The trustees were of the opinion that the building would shortly be conveyed to them and were anxious to proceed with their plans and locate a source of funding for the project.

It was actually February 1876 before the trustees applied to the CDCF. The response from the fund was that they were not prepared to sanction a cash grant until they knew the number of beds that were currently available at the hospital and, if the conversion were to take place, how many beds could be made available to the CDCF for patients from their own area whom they might refer to the hospital for treatment. The part conversion had at this time 150 beds but demand for these beds was such that there were often 200-300 patients awaiting admission during the summer months. The trustees informed the CDCF that beds could be made available to them on the same conditions as applied to the ordinary subscribers and reminded the governors that the cotton districts already partook largely of the benefits of the hospital with many of the clergy in these districts being supplied with 'recommendations' for the relief of poor cotton operatives.[45]

The hospital trustees proposed that, upon receipt of a grant from the fund, the CDCF would receive 80 recommendations to be used at their own discretion.[46] Despite this sweetener the CDCF was not able to sanction a grant as trustees needed to seek permission from the Lord Chancellor to deal with the funds in their possession which, at the time, amounted to £250,000. In the meantime the governors had set up a four man subcommittee to look further into the Buxton application.

Dr Robertson was visited by Mr Edmund Ashworth of the CDCF governors who requested further details of the proposed work at the hospital. Edmund Ashworth J.P., a wealthy businessman, lived at Egerton Hall, Bolton-le-Moor and was influential on the CDCF. He attended the first of many meetings of the hospital trustees in August 1876 and announced that the necessary powers had been granted from the Lord Chancellor so that progress on the grant application could be made. During an organised tour of the building the CDCF governors were impressed by the way the hospital functioned. They were made aware of the constant and increasing pressure for more beds.

They subsequently decided to offer the trustees a grant of £5,000 on the condition that the Duke of Devonshire would relinquish the rest of the building and be supplied with stabling elsewhere. They suggested that the money could be spent on providing 100 extra beds which would be used preferentially by patients referred from the cotton districts at a charge of £1.10s per patient. The grant was at first opposed by the charity commissioners on the grounds that the CDCF should have some form of material guarantee that the money would be spent as intended but this objection was removed when it was agreed that the extra 100 beds would be leased to the CDCF for a period of 100 years at an annual rent of £10.

The long awaited handover of the rest of the building to the hospital trustees came in a letter from Devonshire Buxton agent, George Drewry, to Edmund Ashworth of the CDCF, in which he stated that the duke was prepared to donate the rest of the building providing that he be supplied with suitable replacement stabling. The duke had objected to this move earlier on the grounds that sufficient water could not be supplied to the hospital for the intended baths suite within the building but, now that the charity baths had been built, no such objection remained. With this obstacle out of the way the trustees asked architect Robert Rippon Duke to supply plans and estimates of the probable costs of the extensions.[47]

A meeting of the trustees on 14 April 1877 saw Duke's sketch plans and estimates for the proposed work. Among his recommendations was that the principal entrance to the hospital be made from Devonshire Road with a lodge on either side of the entrance gates. A large stone archway would form the entrance hall, to the right of which would be a waiting room, a sitting room for the Master and Matron, a kitchen and scullery pantry and another set of stairs similar to the ones already in use at the hospital. Also proposed was a consulting room with adjoining waiting room and a series of wards for male patients. The existing consulting room would be used as a nurses room and the existing dining room as a chapel and library for the use of the patients. Cost estimates then followed:

For the conversion of the remainder of the Great stables buildings to the purpose of a hospital	£5,000.
For furnishing and fitting the same	£1,300
Building and finishing of new dining hall	£2,250
Fencing in additional land and laying out ground	£450
Conversion of present sheds to mortuary, improvements to disinfecting room, coal house, wood house, laundry, accident ward departments and fitting up same	£750
Smoking room etc.	£150
Two lodges and entrance gates	£750

This gave a total of £10,650 which was far greater than any of them had imagined and made the CDCF grant of £5000 look immediately inadequate. Despite this the CDCF approved the plans and a memorandum of agreement was set up between the hospital trustees and the CDCF in which the sum of £10,650 would be paid to the trustees in sums not exceeding £2,000 (upon receipt of a certificate from the architect) for the building of the extensions which were to be named The Cotton Districts Wing. The agreement also included a clause that three CDCF governors would become ex-officio members of the committee of management of the hospital for the period of the construction.

Buoyed up by the generosity of the CDCF (and perhaps the prospect of more money from the same source) the architect submitted revised plans to be considered by the board of management. The new plans included the removal of the whole of the internal walls and corridors of the building, thus increasing the space available which could then be used as wards. The colonnade around the open central area would become a means of communication with every part of the hospital, and the open central area, at the suggestion of Dr Robertson, would be glazed over. This scheme would increase the total bed capacity from 250 to 300, a point not lost by the CDCF who would have preferential access to the extra 50 beds.

The revised plans were estimated to cost in the region of £6,000 to £7,000. Accordingly the trustees applied once again to the CDCF (who by now had increased their numbers on the board of management from 3 to 6 representatives) to increase the grant to £18,000. The governors favoured the proposed changes and offered an increased grant of £17,000 and included a proviso that the plans and estimates must be kept within the figure agreed upon since any larger sums might not be obtainable.

Although the figure offered was £1,000 short of that requested, the architect submitted his revised plans in April 1877. These plans included the ambitious idea of covering the whole of the open central area of the building with a dome and were immediately controversial. Dr Flint, one of the resident medical staff, was opposed to the idea on the grounds that covering the central area would reduce the supply of fresh air to the patients, which was regarded as highly efficacious in the treatment of the patients at that time. Some of the governors of the CDCF were opposed to the idea of a dome on cost grounds and others put forward alternative suggestions to roof the area. Mr McClure, of the CDCF, suggested covering the area with a ridge and furrow roof of the type that was used at London Road railway station in Manchester. Other suggestions included filling in the spaces between the stone columns with glazed sashes, thus keeping out the weather whilst still admitting the light, and even one to build an entirely new hospital in the Park.

Duke pressed on doggedly with his dome roof plans and had a valuable ally in Edmund Ashworth who carried some weight amongst his CDCF colleagues. Ashworth was the chairman of the CDCF Building Committee and was in favour of the dome roof from the beginning and, in private discussions with Duke, encouraged the architect to make up sketches of his dome roof as soon as possible so that progress on the matter could be made. The plans were drawn up in secret and, when nearly complete, Duke invited Ashworth to his office in Spring Gardens to examine them. Ashworth was impressed with the sketches and urged the architect to complete the plans and meet him again one week later at the St Pancras Hotel in London. The meeting took place as planned and Ashworth was particularly pleased with the estimate for the work which ranged from £4,000 to £4,250. Ashworth took the plans away with him and promised to return them to Duke in time for his return train to Buxton later that evening. The plans were duly returned and it seems that Duke was given the go-ahead for his project.[48]

It is thought that Ashworth had taken the plans to be independently viewed by a consulting engineer who could rapidly assess the design, practicability and cost. This consultant was most likely Mr Roland Mason Ordish who had established a reputation for this kind of work and who had an office in Great George Street, Westminster. Ordish's obituary in the Engineering magazine said:

> '...*Mr Ordish possessed a remarkable facility for estimating by sight . He would look through a set of contract drawings sent to him for estimating, and after only a few moments' reflection would say "this ought to come out at so many thousand odd pounds." Upon the quantities being taken out by his assistants and the estimate being carefully prepared the result was invariably a remarkably close approximation to his mental estimate...*'[49]

It will be seen later that Mr Ordish may have been further involved in the dome construction.

New Stables

Now that the proposed alterations were almost certainly about to begin, a new site for the duke's Crescent stabling had to be found. The site of the old smithy and premises in the possession of Mr Nall, together with the stables of Messrs Harrison and Le Gros on land north of the railway stations, was thought to be suitable for conversion to this use, and Edmund Ashworth instructed the architect to gain possession of the site if possible. An agreement was reached with the owners and work began on the building of the new stable block in November 1877. The work was completed by May 1878 and was named the Great Livery Stables. The new venture was managed by Messrs Harrison & Le Gros, proprietors of the St Anne's Hotel in the Crescent.

The stabling block on Palace Road which was erected to replace the facilities at the Great Stables for the Duke of Devonshire following the hand over of the whole building for the use of the Buxton Bath Charity.

Plans Agreed and Tenders Sought

In March 1878 the remaining buildings and land at the hospital were formally transferred by the Duke of Devonshire to the trustees for £5000. Trustees now owned all the land upon which the hospital stood with the exception of a plot in the north east corner where local draper and hospital trustee Edward Chambers Milligan owned Northleigh Villas (which were to be bought by the hospital later). All legal arrangements were now in place to allow the trustees to pursue their long standing aim.

The massive rebuilding programme was divided into two parts for the purpose of tendering. Contract No. 1 was for the general building and conversion work, and contract No. 2 for the precision ironwork of the dome. Eighteen firms replied, the cheapest for contract 1 being £21,000 and for contract 2 £4,840, a total of £25,840 which dwarfed the £17,000 grant offered by the CDCF. In an attempt to reduce this figure, the architect abandoned the planned entrance portico and one of the two external lodges which brought down the cost to £23,000.

A frosty response was received from the CDCF to a request for further funding, but Dr Robertson and the architect countered by stating that the planned number of beds could not be provided if they were limited to a £17,000 grant. A period of negotiation, and not a little influence from Mr Ashworth, resulted in the approval of a increase of £7,000, bringing the total to £24,000. The governors made it very clear that this was their maximum grant and no more money would be forthcoming from the fund.

Edmund Ashworth, who had worked tirelessly to persuade his colleagues on the CDCF to provide the grant, wrote to Dr Robertson in August 1879:

'Egerton Hall, Bolton-le-Moors.

Dear Dr Robertson,

After a long conflict, and surrounded by many difficulties, the extension of the Buxton Hospital is now largely carried as far as relates to the mode of doing it and of the provision of the money. The opposition I received from my own building committee, the Governors of the funds and the Charity Committees almost tired me out and made me ready to give it up in disdain... I am happy to say I am relieved now that the last act has been accomplished but the care and the trouble will be thrown upon you and your committee. I hope you took my advice to get a selection of four or five of your best men on the committee to act as a Building Committee along with yourself to see that all the work and contracts (are) faithfully and honestly carried out...' [50]

The Building Committee, chaired by Dr Robertson, consisted of E.C. Milligan (draper and member of the Buxton Local Board), Isaac Walton (bank manager), G.F. Barnard (wine & spirit merchant and member of the Buxton Local Board) and Josiah Taylor (Clerk to the Buxton Local Board). It met every Thursday at 3.00pm., the first meeting being held in September 1879 when it was agreed that the group should report monthly to the board of management on the progress of the works. The tender offered by builder Samuel Warburton, of Manchester, was accepted for contract number 1 and Henry Rankin of Liverpool was awarded contract No. 2. Duke had used the firm of Rankin during the construction of the Pavilion Gardens Concert Hall in 1876 and had direct experience of the quality of their work. [51]

The job of Clerk of works for the project was awarded to Mr Allen Vickers in September 1879 with a payment of £350 for his exclusive services during the full term of the project.

The next two pages show the prospectus for the conversions, dated July 1880. The document outlines all the proposed changes and invites donations towards the cost. Amongst the sketches, showing the building before and after the conversion, is this artist's impression of the completed building with the intended portico entrance and two lodges.

The Governors of the Cotton Districts Convalescent Fund granted the sum of £24,000, to be devoted to the Extension of the Devonshire Hospital, and its mineral water Baths at Buxton, so efficacious in the relief of Rheumatism. By the expenditure of the grant the Wards of the Hospital will be improved and enlarged so as to receive 300 instead of 150 patients; and the central area of half an acre will be covered by a dome to afford space for exercise and recreation in cold and wet weather. In addition to these improvements it has been felt that the original designs of the Architect (Mr. R. R. Duke) should be completed by erecting a Clock Tower, Portico, and another Lodge: most useful in themselves, as a muniment room, for shelter at the principal entrance, and for increased accommodation for out-door servants.

This completion, at a cost of £3,000, it is proposed to effect in recognition of the valuable services of Dr. Robertson, so long connected with the Institution by his medical services, and during so many years holding the position of Chairman of the Committee of Management.

Several views are submitted herewith, in the hope that the numerous friends and benefactors of the Institution may subscribe to this desirable object.

Communications may be sent to any member of the Committee of Management; to the Buxton Branch of the Sheffield and Rotherham Banking Company, the Treasurers of the Hospital; or to Mr. Joseph Taylor, the Secretary, Devonshire Hospital, Buxton, Derbyshire.

Signed on behalf of the Members of the Committee of Management,

WILLIAM MALAM, M.A.,

Vicar of Buxton, Chairman of Special Meetings of the Committee of
Management for carrying out the object in question.

Devonshire Hospital, Buxton, July, 1880.

THE FOLLOWING DONATIONS HAVE ALREADY BEEN PROMISED.

	£	s.	d.
His Grace the Duke of Devonshire, K.G., &c.	200	0	0
Joseph Stockburn, Esq., Kettering	1	1	0
The Rev. Canon Whitelegge, Farnsfield Vicarage, Southwell	1	1	0
Mrs. Hillyard, Oakford Rectory, North Devon	1	1	0
Peter Cadman, Esq., Sheffield	5	0	0
E. W.	2	3	0
Mrs. E. W.	2	2	0
J. Challinor, Esq., Compton, Leek	2	2	0
Miss Margaret Smith, Leek (per Mr. Challinor)	3	0	0
Miss E. Trimmer, Hartley Rectory, Dartford	1	1	0
James Chadwick, Esq., High Bank, Prestwich	100	0	0
Joseph Paget, Esq., Stuffyn Wood, Mansfield	5	0	0
J. W. Taylor, Esq., Summerhill, Buxton	5	5	0
The Misses Lucas, The Brow, Fallowfield	5	0	0
Frederick Cooper, Esq., Inspector-General of Hospitals	20	0	0
The Lady Waterpark, Mapleton, Ashbourne	5	0	0
John J. Marsden, Esq., The Beaufort, Chelsea	2	2	0
S. P. Ashworth, Esq., Headingley, Leeds	1	1	0
William Malkin, Esq., Rock Cliffe, Cheadle, Staffordshire	1	1	0
R. R. Duke, Esq., Buxton	25	0	0
Charles Milner, Esq., Eyre Lane, Sheffield	5	0	0
Messrs. Hodgson & Simpson, Calder Works, Wakefield	1	0	0
In Memory of E. R.	20	0	0
Thomas A. Negus, Esq., Lynn, Walsall	1	1	0
Messrs. R. Wade, Sons, & Co., Hull	10	0	0
Samuel Warburton, Esq., Harpurhey	10	0	0
Messrs. Rankin & Co., Liverpool	5	0	0
Miss Tristram, Settle, Yorkshire	1	1	0
G. H. Leather, Esq., Greenhill, Bingley	5	0	0
W. Carter, Esq., Stoke-on-Trent	1	0	0
Mrs. R. Atkinson, Church House, Aberford	2	2	0

	£	s.	d
The Rev. C. J. Bayley, Christ Church Rectory, Heaton Norris	1	0	0
Mrs. Lewis, Crouch Hill House, Hornsey	1	1	0
Miss Thexton, Buxton	5	0	0
Mrs. Frederick, Park-street, Hull	1	0	0
Richard Wheatley, Esq., Mirfield	1	1	0
The Rev. C. K. Dean, Over Tabley, Knutsford (per Mr. Barnard)	1	1	0
Mrs. White, Plas Warren, Duddleston	5	5	0
Henry Charlewood, Esq., Crumpsall Crescent, Manchester	10	0	0
Sir George Yule, Bayswater, London, W.	5	0	0
Abraham Farrar, Esq., Headingley, Leeds	2	2	0
The Misses Flint, Buxton	2	2	0
The Rev. Father Power, Buxton	1	1	0
Isaac Walton, Esq., Buxton	5	0	0
E. C. Milligan, Esq., Buxton	5	0	0
The Rev. W. Malam, M.A., The Vicarage, Buxton	5	0	0
Miss H. J., Wakefield	10	0	0
Henry Evans, Esq., West Bank, Derby (per Rev. W. Malam)	5	0	0
John Goosey, Esq., Kettering	1	1	0
The Right Rev. Monsignore Canon Thompson, Esh Laude, Durham	2	2	0
G. F. Barnard, Esq., Buxton	5	0	0
J. H. Porteus Oakes, Esq., Nowton Court, Bury St. Edmunds	1	0	0
A. Barnett, Esq., Buxton	5	0	0
The Rev. S. Ray Eddy, M.A., Brindle Rectory	2	2	0
The Rev. C. E. Mayo, Colesgrove, Cheshunt	1	1	0
T. H. Lowthian, Esq., Buxton	5	0	0
Miss Annie Eyre, Penmore House, Chesterfield	2	2	0
The Rev. Augustin Ley, St. Weonards, Ross	2	0	0
Mrs. Aston W. Smith, The Old Hall, Bootle, Liverpool	5	0	0
P. Le Gros, Esq., Buxton	5	0	0
Dr. Dickson, Wye House, Buxton	10	0	0

No. 1.—View of the Devonshire Hospital at Buxton previous to the additions that are now being made.

No. 2.—Plan of the Hospital and Grounds as enlarged.

No. 3.—View of the Hospital as now being enlarged by the grant of £24,000 from the Cotton Districts Convalescent Fund.

No. 4.—View of the Devonshire Hospital as proposed to be completed by the further expenditure of £3,000, now asked for.

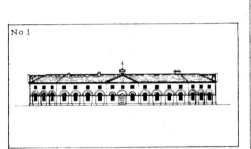

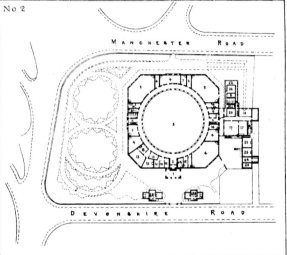

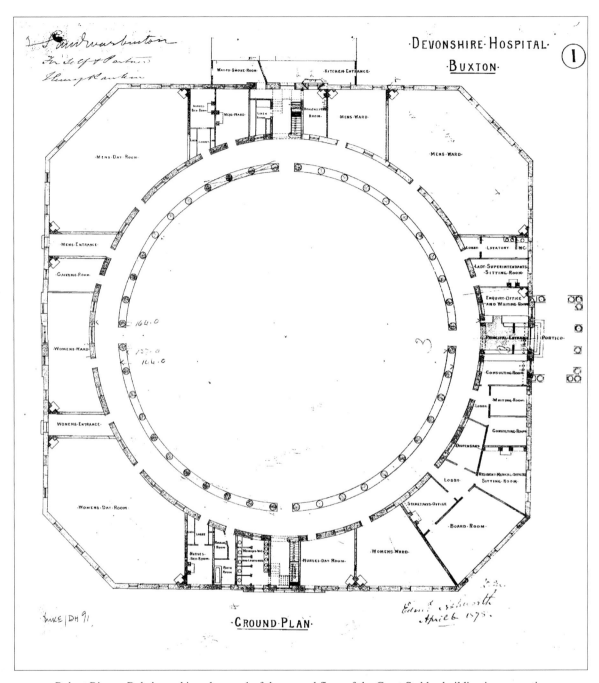

Robert Rippon Duke's working plan no. 1 of the ground floor of the Great Stables building in preparation for the full conversion to a hospital. The two separate entrances from Manchester Road for male and female patients can be seen on the left side of the plan.

Work Begins

Work commenced in September 1879 and almost immediately it was discovered that the the parts of the building upon which the dome was to rest were unsatisfactory and the ironwork would need to be redesigned with extra strengtheners. Rankin agreed to carry out this work at no extra cost to the trustees. Existing plans show that the dome and its supports were changed several times in order to spread the load correctly on the circular entablature supported by the circle of stone pillars which surround the open area.

The wrought iron skeleton of the dome was an early contribution to the project and must have been a sight to behold for Buxton's residents who would not have seen its like before. Recent research on the construction of the dome has suggested that the architect R.R. Duke, and his iron fabricating firm Messrs Henry Rankin of Liverpool, may not have had the mathematical knowledge to calculate the loadings on all parts of the ironwork to design the dome in detail. Certainly the precision of its construction was a matter of great concern to the architect and it is possible that the engineer, R.M. Ordish, provided or advised upon the calculations needed. An obituary for Ordish says that he was '...*engaged on the Buxton Sanatorium...*' [52] which must mean the Devonshire Hospital and ties in with the earlier possible involvement of this eminent engineer in the design. [53] R.R. Duke visited Rankin's Liverpool iron foundry to see the construction of the large supporting wrought iron ribs that were to support the dome, and said of it:

> '...*When the making of the large ribs of the iron roof commenced I went to the works to see them set out full-size, and was pleased at the way the master and his foremen set about the work, being anxious to have a true curve, as it would be seen from a distance on all sides. I went several times, and saw the first rib put together in a suitable timber frame or mould fixed to ground, and felt satisfied that all would be precisely the same. I kept this part of the work entirely in my own hands; all the other trades I left with the clerk of works...*' [54]

Each of the supporting ribs was to be attached at the base of the dome to a continuous wrought iron ring, seated on top of the circular entablature so that the weight of the roof exerted its forces directly downwards with no lateral pressure which could force the columns apart. In the event this was not considered to be a strong enough arrangement and later alterations to the plans include the introduction of iron buttresses which span the distance from the base of each rib to the surrounding wall in order to strengthen the whole structure.

The Tay Bridge Disaster

During the fixing of the ribs Duke ascended the scaffolding every day to personally supervise the erection. It was his habit during these visits to take luncheon at the Palace Hotel. On one of these visits he met with a railway engineer, Mr Footner, who told him of his recent visit to see the fallen Tay Bridge and outlined his opinions on the bridge's inherent weaknesses.

The bridge, spanning the Firth of Tay in Perth was opened in 1878 by the North British Railway, and designed by the architect Sir Thomas Bouch (1822-1880). It was built in a lattice girder design at a length of 3,459 yards and at a height of 88 feet from the river bed. It collapsed on December 8th 1879 as the Edinburgh mail train was passing resulting in the loss of some 75 lives. No allowance had been made in the design of the bridge for undue stresses being placed on it in high winds and lateral wind bracing had not been built into the bridge.

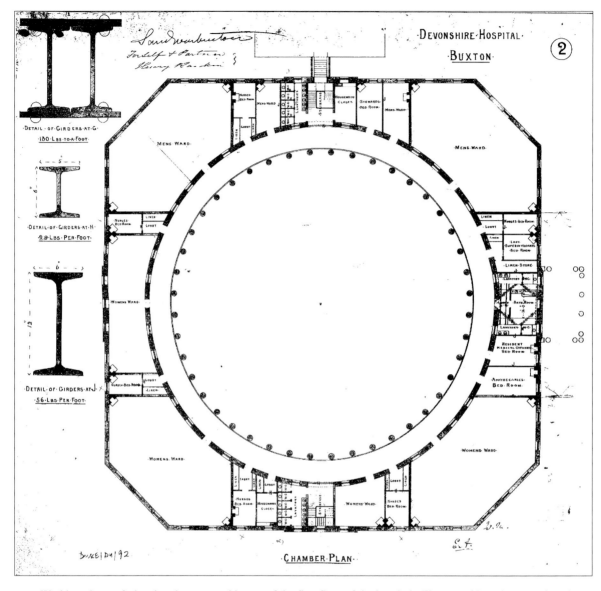

Working plan no.2 showing the proposed layout of the first floor of the hospital. These working plans are signed by Samuel Warburton and by Henry Rankin who signs 'for self and partner'

Mr Footner's description obviously affected Duke as he went straight back to inspect the roof where men were still erecting the dome ribs. On inspection he noted that the bolt holes of the rib sections were not correctly in line and, in order to fix the sections, the men were 'drifting' or hammering the bolts in to connect holes together. In one case they were unable to drift so they heated a bolt to red heat in order to drive it in through the mismatched holes. Duke ordered them to stop this procedure immediately and decided to have the ribs redrilled and the bolts made to fit. This would undoubtedly have been most unpopular amongst the men, particularly since drifting was common practise in this kind of work and, although undesirable, had less effect on the integrity of a wrought iron structure than one of steel. [55]

The weight of the dome exerts massive forces downwards and outwards on the building beneath it. These forces need to be managed in such a way that the stress is transferred directly down and thus preventing the supporting walls from being pushed apart. The original intention was to have the dome resting on the entablature of the circular columns but, as this photograph shows, extra strengthening was required in the form of cast iron arched girders which traverse the space between the stone entablature and the inner wall.

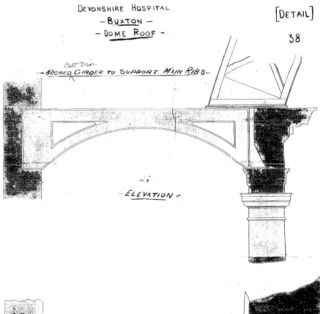

DEVONSHIRE HOSPITAL
- BUXTON -
- DOME ROOF -

[DETAIL]

38

ARCHED GIRDER TO SUPPORT MAIN RIBS

- ELEVATION -

- PLAN -

- SCALE 1 INCH TO A FOOT -

R.R. Duke's detailed plans showing how the base of the main rib projects beyond the stone entablature and rests partly on the arched girder.

Progress at the Hospital

By July 1880 a great part of the project had been completed and *The Builder* magazine of 10 July 1880 described the extent of the progress:

> '...*Very large extensions have been made to this building under the direction of Mr R. R. Duke, Architect.*
>
> *The superficial area now provided for wards is as follows;- for males 11,614 superficial feet; for females 10,912 superficial feet thus providing accommodation for 300 patients.*
>
> *The outer form of the hospital is an irregular octagon with an inner circular area of 164 feet diameter; within this there is a circle of columns 138 feet in diameter forming a colonnaded 13 feet wide all around the inner area. These columns with their entablature rise 25 feet above the floor and from this panel springs the dome covering the whole of this area. The dome is formed of wrought iron ribs, 22 principal ones and 22 intermediate ones secured at the foot to a wrought iron rim and heavy cast iron girders connecting the inner area wall and the colonnade and thus securing a perfectly firm base for the dome. The ribs rise to a height of 50 feet from the base or 75 feet from the floor line and are there secured to a wrought iron ring 40 feet in diameter from which springs a lantern light also having a 40 feet diameter and being 18 feet high thus giving a total height from floor to roof lantern of 93 feet and to top of finial of 118 feet,*
>
> *In addition to the lantern light above named there are 8 other skylights on the roof at the base of the dome; and together they give 4,500 feet superficial light to the central hall. The superficial area of this hall is just half an acre; and is capable of holding 6,000 people. Its cubic contents are about one million of feet, a remarkable work...*' [56]

In July 1880 a lightning conductor was attached to the iron ribs of the dome to protect the building. By September the north wing and kitchen were virtually complete and the patients were moved into the new part of the building so that their existing ward areas could be made available to the contractor.

Ventilation of the building was addressed by the fitting of a 'Boyle's patent air pump' on the lantern above the dome. The expenditure of an additional £300 was sanctioned by the trustees in September on the extension of the new laundry by the erection of a wood and glass structure in front of it. The October 1880 meeting of the trustees accorded a vote of thanks to the architect and a visitor to the town, a Mr Crosby, for extinguishing a small fire in the new extension.

Delays in the Contract

The contractors for the project were paid in £2,000 instalments upon the issuing of a payment certificate by the architect when he was satisfied that the work had been completed. Warburton made an application in December 1880 for the ninth instalment of the grant as work could not proceed until the money was available. [57]

Duke felt that Warburton could carry on the work without issuing a certificate for the full £2,000 instalment and advised the committee to issue a draft for £500 only. This was agreed to and Warburton had to settle with a lower sum until the required amount of work had been completed to warrant the issue of the next instalment. This did not meet with Warburton's approval - he complained that the progress of the work was delayed by committee bureaucracy. He wrote to the architect demanding that £1000 should be paid to him from the retention money held by the trustees because he had been seriously held up by not having full possession of the building when required. This was a prelude to the arguments put in the protracted arbitration case which arose towards the end of the contract.

A further disagreement between Warburton and Duke, in February 1881, added to the controversy. This was regarding the price to be paid for making good deficiencies in the large beams of the main building. Warburton wanted to be paid 2s.6d. per cubic foot for the timbers, a price thought much too high by the architect. Rankin, the iron-man, offered to sell the timber he was using as scaffolding under the dome at 1 shilling per foot, which was far more realistic. Advice had to be taken regarding the legality of the purchase from this source and, having received an assurance from their solicitors the trustees authorised the purchase from Rankin at great savings to themselves. In addition it was decided that local builder, Mr James Salt's tender for carting, sawing and fixing, including labour and nails should be accepted for the sum of 8d per cubic foot.[58] Salt's tender for the stonework in the circular windows at £25 was also accepted in preference to Warburton's tender of £44 for the same work. This would undoubtedly have annoyed Warburton but it seems that he realised he had been outmanoeuvred when in March 1881 he finally agreed to take on the work of making good the timbers purchased from Rankin at a lower price than that offered by Salt.[59]

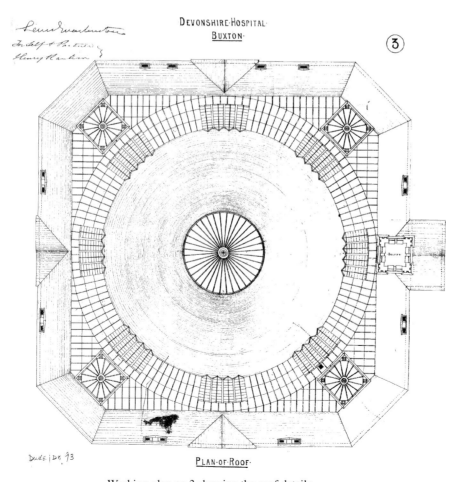

Working plan no.3 showing the roof details.

Later in March Warburton was again urgently applying for a further payment from the trustees on account of his contract and the tone of his letter conveys the sense that he felt ill-used by the committee.

'Dear Sir'

Mr Denton has sent me a copy of a form of receipt which I understand your committee wish me to sign before receiving any more money. I don't see that existing circumstances require any special form of acknowledgement for payment of money. It seems that if I sign a receipt for the money on account of work done and material supplied to the hospital it will answer every proposal without compromising the committee in any way. Considering that I have been impeded to such a large extent by not having possession of the old building, waiting for iron work and other causes, I think I am entitled to this. You are no doubt aware that my contract contains no provision for the building being given up to me in sections or finishing one portion ready for occupation before another one was given up to me and when I learned after I commenced the works several weeks that this was the intention of the committee I was greatly surprised. This has not only caused great delay but seriously increased cost to me has also occurred for which I ought to be compensated. I shall be much obliged if you will kindly place the matter before the committee and I hope that they will at once forward a cheque to my address for £2,000.

I am Dear Sir, Your Servant
Samuel Warburton...' [60]

Certainly, if the contents of Warburton's letter were an accurate reflection of the state of things, it is difficult to not have some sympathy for his predicament. The question of not having complete possession of the building must have had a significant braking effect on the works, but it seems that the trustees maintained their indifferent air and showed little sympathy to Warburton's plight in agreeing to issue him with a cheque for £1,500 later that month. [61]

A meeting of the trustees held on 31 March 1881 discussed the issue of additional unforeseen expenses which amounted to another £2,000. The charity did not have any resources to meet this shortfall and therefore decided to once again apply to the CDCF to make up this difference. The CDCF had made their position on the granting of any extra money very clear at the issuing of the £24,000 grant and it must have been with great reluctance that the trustees made this request. The CDCF gave their response in May when Mr McClure advised the trustees that the fund was heavily involved in the administration of a grant to Southport Hospital and advised them to apply later in the year when their application was more likely to be favourably looked upon.

Charity Drinking Well

As part of the overall project the committee discussed the problem of overcrowding at the public drinking well at the Natural Baths. The problem had been in evidence for some time and the extension programme gave the trustees an ideal opportunity to include the erection of a purpose built drinking well for the exclusive use of the charity patients. The Charity Drinking Well was designed by Robert Duke and sited in the yard adjoining the western end of the 1876 charity hot baths in George Street, and was opened on 1 August 1882. The new building offered more spacious and comfortable surroundings and ample seating was provided for the more infirm. The building features Italianate windows and a pedimented roof which matches the design of the Devonshire Hospital. Incised in the stonework above the arch on the west elevation is '...*Devonshire Hospital Drinking*

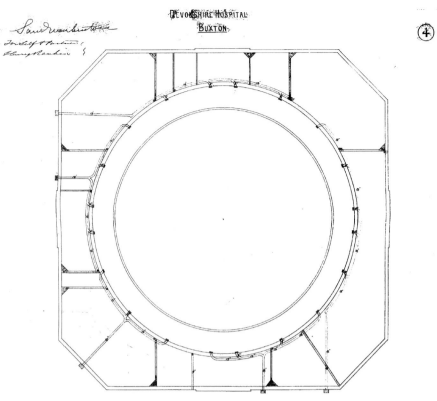

Working plan no.4 gives the layout of the ground floor ventilation.

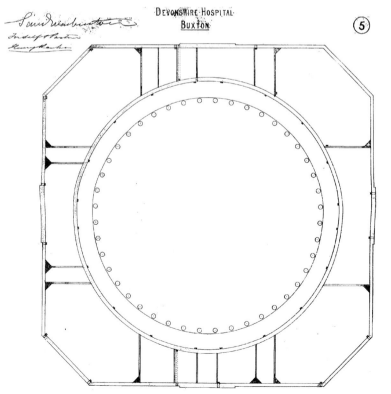

Working plan no.5 showing the ventilation details for the Chamber or first floor.

Well A.D. 1882...' and on the south front '...*St Ann's Well Water Pump Room, For Devonshire Hospital Patients only...*'[62]

In the provision of this pump room the charity patients had their own new facility well before the new paying pump room was opened in the Crescent in 1894.

Charity Drinking Well on the corner of George Street and adjacent to the Charity Natural Bath building. Erected in 1882, this well provided mineral water drinking facilities for the charity patients who had previously used the drinking well in the Natural Baths to the west of the Crescent.

Slow Progress at the Hospital

A deadline for the completion of the project had been set for August 1881 but by May concern was being expressed at the lack of progress being made. The architect was concerned that the dome lantern was still unfinished and the slating of the dome roof had not even commenced. He urged the contractor's foreman, Mr Havender, to take on extra men to advance the work. Havender agreed to set on twelve slaters and four glaziers immediately in attempt to complete by the allotted date. He was offered the incentive of £5 if he were able to finish by the end of the first week in August or £10 if he completed by the first day of August. Warburton was again requesting further payments on account in June but the committee resolved to delay the issuing of another payment certificate for £1,000 until significant progress had been made on the slating of the dome. The frequent delays to the project were set out in *The Buxton Advertiser*:

> '...*The height and proposed position of the dome and roof of the buildings often renders the work dangerous or impossible, and especially during frost, snow or windy weather. Every allowance will be made for the delays thus occasioned. The extent of the works is another adequate reason for delay in the completion. The weight of the iron alone, in the dome itself is 352 tons, the weight of the other materials employed in the construction of the dome, including slate, glass, wood and plaster is stated to be 235 tons - a total weight of 560 tons. The plastering etc. of these overhanging surfaces at so great an elevation requires such care that the men have had to be accustomed gradually to the work, to lessen the risk of serious accident. All these circumstances must be taken into consideration before blame is laid upon any of those concerned in carrying out this large undertaking and, in many respects, novel construction. The principal delay seems to be due to the difficulty in obtaining slates of the necessary size for the different courses around the great circuit of the dome. The end, however of such hindrances must be near at hand; and in the course of the next few weeks the completion of the undertaking may be probably expected...*'[63]

The heating to the building was installed using hot water pipes which passed under the floors, with coils of piping under the wards and day rooms, whereas smaller rooms were heated by pipes placed above the floor. The large central hall had six rows of pipes fixed around its circumference, four rows above the floor and two under the gallery. Ventilation was achieved through a series of 12 inch earthenware pipes passing under the floor and branching off to each ward and the colonnade with their ends open to the outside of the building. Internally the pipes were connected to specially constructed wooden shafts which were attached vertically to the walls to a height of 8 feet. Although box shaped, these were referred to as 'Tobin tubes' by the architect. The open coal fires, which were used to heat the wards, needed a plentiful supply of air to ensure efficient burning. From July onwards the work seemed to be progressing rapidly, so much so that Warburton and Duke felt that the reopening of the hospital could take place at the end of August and informed the trustees to make the necessary arrangements with that date in mind.

A meeting of the trustees held in September once again discussed the possibility of applying to the CDCF for extra money. The cost of the project had now risen by £3,200 above the original grant. Doubts were expressed that the fund would sanction a further grant and it was felt that the Charity Commissioners would probably block the payment of further monies. Consequently the committee decided to let the work be completed and pay the shortfall using precious hospital funds. The architect's personal notebook records estimates for the work done during extensions:

Building and extensions	£21,787. 13s. 5d
Heating Apparatus	1,332. 17s. 8d
Architect	1,200. 0s. 0d
Clerk of Works	427. 10s. 0d
General repairs to extension of old buildings	266. 16s. 0d.
Total	£25,014. 17s. 1d

Included in the above figure was the dome roof as follows:

Iron work	£2,780. 0s 0d
All other work as carpenters plumber, glazer, slater, painter, etc.	£1,496. 13s 6d
Total	£4,276. 13s. 6d [64]

He also records the cost of the new Charity Baths on George Street at £1018, the clock tower at £1034, furniture and fittings at £1282, and laying out of the grounds at £366, giving a grand total of £28,715. It will be seen in chapter three that the final total was considerably higher than this calculation.

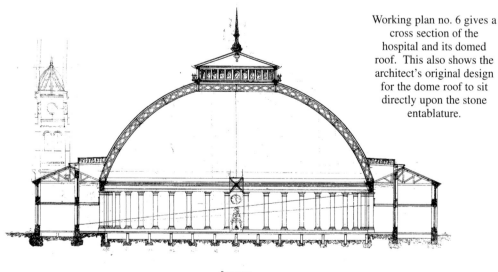

Working plan no. 6 gives a cross section of the hospital and its domed roof. This also shows the architect's original design for the dome roof to sit directly upon the stone entablature.

·SECTION·

Dome Statistics

The Devonshire dome, unlike some other dome constructions, does not rely upon the integral strength of the materials in the membrane of the shell, rather its strength derives from a series of radially disposed ribs. In this it is more closely analogous to a conventional parallel arch iron rib vault of the type frequently found in the mid 19th century in the construction of large span roofs used in railway station train sheds. The arched iron framework provides the strength and the outer shell has only a marginal part to play in the structural rigidity. However, the dome may be unique in being the only known roof of this type to be constructed on a pre-existing base - the Georgian riding stables.

When the dome was completed it was found that it deviated from its planned position by no more than one eighth of an inch which was a tribute to all concerned. The distance between the internal columns supporting the dome is 138 feet and the maximum diameter of the dome is 145 feet - not the 156 feet which has often been quoted in other writings. The erroneous 156 feet figure probably originated from the Engineer magazine which said: '...*The dome is a segment of a sphere, the diameter of which is 156 feet 6 inches...*' [65] This has been taken to mean that this figure is the dome's diameter but it is important to realise that the dome is rather less than a hemisphere and the base of the dome is considerably higher than the point where the maximum diameter of the sphere would be, making the diameter of the dome base less.

Other writers have used the figure of 164 feet but this is actually the internal diameter of the hospital's ground floor which extends well beyond the circumference of the dome. In a league table of domes it is slightly smaller than the Pantheon, Rome (142 feet) but is roughly comparable to the dome over the British Library Reading Room (1849) at 140 feet and smaller than the Royal Albert Hall dome which has a maximum diameter of 219 feet. Other comparisons have been made with St Peter's Rome (138 feet), the Duomo, Florence (137 feet) and St Paul's London (112 feet).

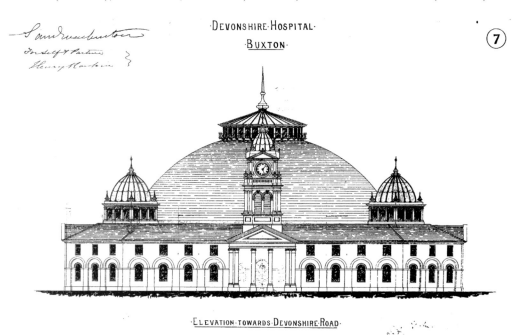

·DEVONSHIRE·HOSPITAL·
·BUXTON·

⑦

·ELEVATION·TOWARDS·DEVONSHIRE·ROAD·

Working plan no.7 is an elevation of the hospital as seen from Devonshire road which includes the proposed clock tower and grand portico entrance. A lack of funds prevented the construction of the portico.

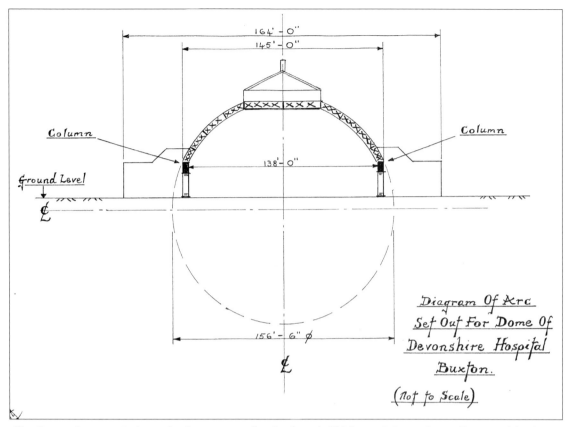

The distance between the internal columns supporting the dome is 138 feet and the maximum diameter of the dome is 145 feet. This drawing also shows where the frequently misquoted figure of 156 feet, the diameter of the full hemisphere is derived, and that of 164 feet which is actually the internal diameter of the hospital's ground floor, an area which extends well beyond the circumference of the dome.

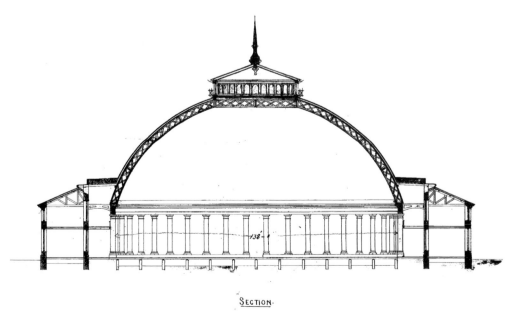

SECTION·

This cross section may be compared with that on page 49. It shows the modified design where the dome roof now sits partly on arched girders surrounding the dome base in order to increase its stability.

Completion of the Works and Preparations for the Grand Opening

As the work neared completion the architect submitted designs for two marble tablets to be erected at the hospital's main entrance. The tablets were installed on either side of the entrance and can still be seen today; one tablet lists the names of the Governors of the CDCF and the other, the trustees and committee of management of the Devonshire Hospital. From 1869 the hospital had acquired the services of an Honorary Meteorologist, who used a meteorological station in the grounds, and during the conversion, a new small building, in the grounds for this purpose was designed by R.R. Duke.

The Duke of Devonshire was invited to re-open the hospital at the end of August. It was known that the Prince of Wales was due to visit Liverpool on 6 September and the invitation contained a suggestion that he may like to use his influence to invite the Prince to perform the opening. In the event the Prince of Wales was fully committed with engagements and the duke could not be available until October. It was decided that the grand opening would take place on Tuesday 11 October 1881, being the most convenient date for all concerned. The duke would be at Chatsworth on the 10th and proposed to arrive in Buxton the following day at 11.00am and would need to leave for Manchester at 3.30pm.

Each subscriber to the charity was issued with a copy of a circular showing sketches of the exterior and interior of the hospital printed by the proprietor of the *Buxton Advertiser*, John Cumming Bates, with the approval of the architect on matters of architectural detail. Copies of the same circular were to be made available for sale to the public, at one penny, on the day of the opening. Invitations were sent to:

> The Chairman & governors of the CDCF
> President & trustees of the hospital
> Chairman and members of the Local Board
> Directors of the Buxton Improvements Company
> Local magistrates
> Clergy and ministers of the various churches and places of worship in the neighbourhood
> The medical gentlemen of Buxton
> Chairman of the School Board
> Principals of the two leading schools
> Chairman of the Midland and London North Western Railway Companies and other such donors and friends of the institution as the committee considered desirable.

An entrance fee of one shilling per person was determined and the Buxton Improvements Company accepted an invitation to bring along their band to play suitable music during and after the ceremony. The opening ceremony was advertised in the London daily papers, the medical papers and the Manchester, Liverpool, Leeds Bradford, Sheffield, Derby, Chesterfield, Halifax and Buxton papers. The trustees met with the masters of both railway stations who agreed to lay on extra trains on the day of the opening.

Messrs Harrison & Le Gros of the St Anne's Hotel declined to provide the luncheon under the conditions specified by the trustees and it was decided to offer the contract to Messrs Jefferson of Manchester. Jefferson's replied that they were unable to supply a luncheon for less than 7s 6d per head and eventually the contract was awarded to Mr Sandilands, of the Palace Hotel, who offered to serve lunch for 4s per head providing that a minimum of 200 guests could be guaranteed. He would also supply luncheon to the musicians at 1s. per head and arrange all the tables and a platform for the speakers.

During construction the dome skeleton is here photographed from Manchester Road.

Interior photograph during the construction of the dome. The wooden scaffolding shown here was later used for construction work in the conversion project.

A deputation from the Liberal club approached the board to enquire whether the Duke of Devonshire would be prepared to include a visit to their club in Spring Gardens whilst he was in Buxton but Dr Robertson turned them down as the duke had only a limited amount of time in the town and would be fully occupied at the hospital.

The London Illustrated News offered to include an illustration of the building in their paper if sketches were available. A copy of a lithograph of the extension was duly sent and the architect agreed to have a photograph of the interior of the building taken for inclusion. Newspaper reporters were invited to a meeting of the committee of management with the governors scheduled for 11.00am on the day of the opening. The Local Board were also making their own arrangements for the day, deciding to meet at 10.30am at the Board office and walk from there to the hospital.

Local tradesmen were asked to close their shops from 11am to 3 pm. The chairman of the Local Board, Edward Milligan, felt that the town should spend more money on occasions such as this and was in favour of the use of electric lighting as had been recently used at the northern resort of Blackpool.

A most unusual view of the hospital as seen from the roof of the nearby Palace Hotel.

The Opening Ceremony

The trustees met at the hospital at 8.30am on the morning of the 11 October to finalise the details of the day's proceedings. As with many open air events in Buxton, the weather was threatening and rain looked likely. Mr Arthur Willoughby, manager of the Pavilion Gardens, organised the formation of a procession consisting of the Chapel-en-le-Frith volunteer band, Queen of the Peak fire engine & brigade, Buxton old fire engine & brigade, Duke of Devonshire Lodge of Oddfellows, Whaley Bridge Volunteer Band, Buxton local schoolchildren and the Board School, and Sunday School children from Burbage and Fairfield.

The procession began at about 10.00am on the Market Place and proceeded along High Street, West Road, Broad Walk, The Crescent, Spring Gardens, Bridge Street and returned back through Spring Gardens and the Quadrant to the Midland Railway station. The procession divided at the Post Office with the fire brigades moving on to the station and the remainder to the hospital.

Robert Rippon Duke (1817-1909)

The Duke of Devonshire arrived at the station at 11.00am and was transported by carriage to the hospital, the route having been festooned with bunting supplied by Mr Bachoffner of Leeds. The duke was met at the hospital by the architect and Dr Robertson. The key of the main entrance was handed by the architect to the duke who opened the main door and entered the newly converted hospital. The architect answered the duke's questions about the marble slabs at the entrance and the party moved on to the board room for a meeting with the committee of management and the Governors of the CDCF. A formal meeting was held with the duke in the chair where statements of the building accounts were presented and found to be in order. The calculations at that time showed that twelve instalments of grant from the CDCF had been received but that when the work was fully completed and paid for the hospital would be left with a deficiency of £3,135.

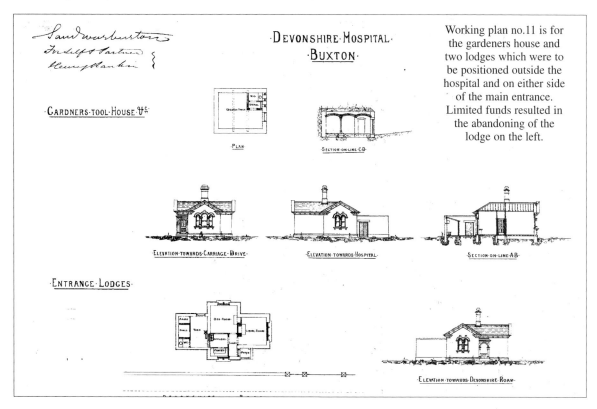

Working plan no.11 is for the gardeners house and two lodges which were to be positioned outside the hospital and on either side of the main entrance. Limited funds resulted in the abandoning of the lodge on the left.

After the meeting the duke was shown around the building by the architect, the chairman of the trustees and members of the hospital management committee. The house surgeon read out case histories of some of the Lancashire patients who had been treated at the hospital. Upon returning to the board room, the duke expressed his satisfaction with the admirable way in which the project had been carried out, before they adjourned to the central hall under the great dome and the assembled public.

The hospital chaplain, Rev. W Malam offered prayers and the duke addressed the public declaring the new hospital officially open. Mr Hugh Mason MP and governor of the CDCF spoke in support and appreciation of the extensions and Dr Robertson then read an address on the value of the hospital charity in times past.

The band played the National Anthem and the company sat down to the luncheon. After lunch, Dr Robertson made another speech, taking the opportunity to mention the cash deficiency of just over £3,000 needed to complete the work which he was confident could be raised by public donation. With the official proceedings over, the grand firework display commenced outside the hospital. The weather lived up to expectations and rain fell on the display, dampening the squibs, but having no effect whatsoever on those involved in the venture who would have felt justifiably proud to be there on the day of the great opening.

At the end of the year, the *Buxton Advertiser* gave its usual coverage of the events of the year, a year of some importance to the town, and inevitably included some column inches about the hospital project. A small extract will crystallise progress thus far as we move on to record further strides in the life and work of the hospital:

> '... *This great hospital business is the event of the year, however it may have been brought about. It is the greatest testament that the Buxton waters have received in no insubstantial manner and shows Buxton, in the future, will owe much to a great duke and a little duke also...*' [66]

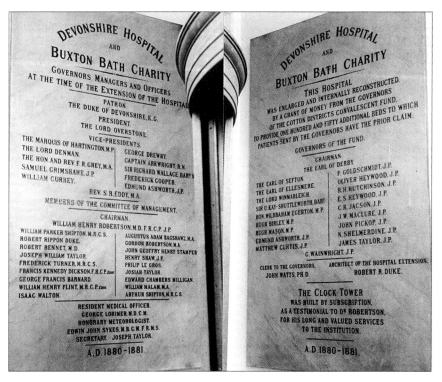

Marble slabs on each side of the entrance to the hospital giving details of all those involved in the conversion of 1879-82.

CHAPTER THREE
A reputation is forged

Buxton now had the hospital for which it had longed, and the trustees could be justly proud of a 300 bed provision for the sick poor. It was more than a match for its northern rival Harrogate where the charity hospital would not see any rebuilding until 1889 and then would provide only half the number of beds available at Buxton. Dr W.H. Robertson had led the other doctors in seeing much hard work come to fruition, the potential to establish a national reputation in the treatment of diseases of the 'locomotor' and 'nervous' systems - a centre of excellence - was now in their grasp. [67]

The whole town would benefit from this investment. According to the architect's notebook, the total cost of conversion was £28,715, which included the new Hot Baths, the clock tower, furniture and fittings, and the laying out of the grounds. [68] However, later calculations put the figure at £35,710 and, with the Cotton Districts Convalescent Fund (CDCF) resolutely opposed to a request for further funds, the trustees had no choice but to sell £3,000 worth of consols held by the hospital and to engage in serious fundraising over the following twelve years in order to pay off the debt. [69]

The Hospital Clock

The clock tower was the subject of a separate appeal launched in March 1880 when a further £3000 was sought to augment the £24,000 obtained from the Cotton Districts Convalescent Fund. The proposal was to complete the hospital according to the original plans of the architect providing, an entrance portico and a second lodge as well as a clock tower, this being the wishes of Dr W.H. Robertson, the long-time chairman of the Committee of Management, who was most diffident about the clock tower being provided as a testimonial to his work.[70]

The appeal was unsuccessful in raising the full amount but the clock tower was completed in 1882 by Warburton at a cost of just over £1000, the architect's fee being £50, and, despite his demur, it was dedicated to Dr Robertson and referred to as the 'Robertson Tower' by the local press.[71] It is of Italianate style in keeping with other details by R.R. Duke on the hospital conversion and has been described in two parts or stages. The first stage has paired corner pilasters flanking twin round-headed louvred openings; the upper stage has the clock faces beneath a triangular pediment. The whole structure is surmounted by a lead covered dome.[72]

Such was the financial position of the hospital, however, that there was no money left to buy a clock to put in it! Henry Shaw DL, JP, the son of a Blackburn brewer who had built Corbar Hall, lived in some style at Whitehall, Buxton and he expressed a willingness to donate a clock if the architect would obtain tenders and select a suitable model. Though Shaw was very anxious to have the honour of making this donation to the hospital he was insistent that it should be the property of the Local Board who would have free access to it at all times for winding and maintenance. His reason for this was because of the acrimony between himself and Dr Robertson whom, he said, treated him very badly and tried to snub him on every occasion.[73] This may have arisen from the fact that Henry Shaw was a prominent Congregationalist in town whereas Robertson was a high Anglican, but, whatever might be the reason, Shaw's conditional offer was unacceptable.

Yet again the Duke of Devonshire's generosity saved the day, and the Buxton agent, George Drewry, arranged for the architect to obtain a clock at a cost of £467 and installed for another £69.

The clock has four glazed dials, (one of which directly faces the dome and cannot be read at any angle from the ground) each six feet in diameter, and four bells, tuned to the notes D,C,B flat and F, which chime the Cambridge quarters. The F bell is used for striking the hours and weighs 15 hundredweight. The pendulum has a two hundredweight bob and is compensated in such a way that regardless of temperature the effective length of the pendulum remains the same, thus increasing the clock's accuracy. At its installation, the clock was guaranteed to keep time within ten minutes a month. The clock was made by the firm of Johnson & Son of Queen Street, Derby and has an escapement based on designs by Sir Edmund Beckett who designed the escapement for the clock at the Houses of Parliament.

Flooring and other timber work had to be constructed to house the clock's works and bells, which were installed during the summer months of 1883. The installation was to include a special automatic apparatus which would turn the gas lighting of the face up and down to match the varying lengths of day throughout the year. Initially a small charge was made for the gas but by a Parliamentary Order of 1886 a free supply was obtained.[74]

The official ceremony of starting the clock was at 5.00pm on 10 August, Dr Robertson and George Drewry jointly conducting this, whilst the architect, Robert R. Duke, unable to attend due to poor health, watched the proceedings from his garden on Manchester Road.[75] In 1895 R.R. Duke paid for an oak board to be fixed in the clock tower containing the names of all the subscribers to its building fund.

Argument and Arbitration

Such a bold and imaginative initiative as the hospital conversion was bound to find critics, especially since it had been widely described in the technical journals and general press. One correspondent to *The British Medical Journal*, in a detailed polemic, argued that the conversion was ill-conceived, a waste of money and that the dome, which he described as of 'Brobdignagian' (sic) proportions, was a rather useless covered space which would cost a small fortune to heat. The article went on to suggest that the workmanship was so bad that water leaked down the walls when it rained and patients were nearly blown out of bed by the down-draughts through the building! The estimated total cost of £29,000 and builder's extras of £3,000 could, it was argued, have been much better spent on the provision of a new building.[76]

Of course these criticisms were answered by Dr W.H. Robertson who offered, in his own terms, 'an unqualified contradiction' refuting in detail the points made and citing the architect, the medical resident (Dr George Lorimer) and the secretary (Mr Joseph Taylor) in support of his facts. The 'correspondent', who did not give a name, was conceivably a member of the editorial staff, and had the last word when he described the building as hybrid, being neither stable, hospital or conservatory, but having some of the qualities of all three! [77]

Such a sceptic was unlikely to faze Dr Robertson and his management committee who were immensely proud of the new hospital. The question of builder's extras was, however, an issue which exercised the mind of the architect and trustees for some time. Samuel Warburton had experienced many difficulties with the architect during building and felt that he had been treated shabbily throughout the contract. His grievances came to a head in January 1882 when he sent in a claim for £1,100 to the hospital building committee for compensation for the delays caused to him by not having access to the whole of the hospital during the contract. In addition to the compensation claim he made a claim for what he considered to be extra works beyond those specified in the contract. The recollection of the architect was that he offered £500 to settle all claims but this was refused by Warburton who said, very disdainfully, that he should expect nearer £5000. With this Warburton submitted his accounts to an arbitrator.

The architect was of the opinion that many of the items of extra work submitted by Warburton were not outside the terms of the contract and thus should incur no extra charge. The committee of management employed the services of George Fox, a Manchester solicitor, who advised that the extra work be calculated and a detailed account be forwarded to the builder in the hope that he might moderate his demands. In the event Samuel Warburton would not back down and the two parties agreed to use the same arbitrator, Mr Charles Jackson of Manchester. It was also agreed that, as the dispute was one of measurement and value only, no solicitors, surveyors or valuers should appear at any of the meetings. The schedules and prices were already in the hands of Jackson and it was agreed that the architect and Warburton should personally conduct their own side of the case. All of these measures would save costs for both parties, a serious consideration for the cash-strapped hospital.[78] Thus began a long and protracted case which would not be satisfactorily concluded until the early part of 1884. It would also cause the breakdown in health of the architect and the subsequent decision to sell his business.[79]

Meanwhile, despite the opening of the hospital, work was still underway to complete the conversion. Warburton was now denying any liability to finish the extension works in accordance with instructions issued from the trustees but, in view of the fact that an arbitration procedure had been initiated, he agreed to continue with the remaining work as directed by the architect, and the question of liability would be settled afterwards by Charles Jackson. Attempts to settle the builder's £1100 claim for delays with an offer of £350 came to naught.

Relationships between builder and architect, never easy, were not improved by the criticism of later work done by Warburton as shoddy. Roof work had been completed so unsatisfactorily that recent storms had damaged it resulting in a further claim against the builder. The architect found it necessary to complete and alter some flues in the extensions which had been left by the contractor in a very unsatisfactory state. It was estimated that the work needing to be done would involve altering nearly all the flues installed and would take almost two months to complete with the present number of men. The architect took a unilateral decision to directly employ men to finish the works, again submitting the account to the arbitrator. Members of the hospital management committee were not pleased and the architect was directed to obtain the sanction of the committee before any further additional work was undertaken.

Arbitration proceeded very slowly. Meetings were held at the hospital and at Mr Jackson's office in Manchester. The first meetings, held in March and April 1882, put forward Warburton's evidence in support of his claim and the evidence of his foreman, Mr Havender, and both of them were cross-examined by the architect. Further meetings were held up to August after which an interval of eleven months passed before the next meeting on 18 July 1883 in Manchester. The reason for this long delay in the negotiations was the poor state of health of the architect which is in evidence throughout the whole length of the arbitration. Despite being, at times, bedridden the architect insisted that only he could handle the technical arguments required, this meant that meetings were frequently postponed.

When the architect was well enough to attend the meetings in Manchester he was

Devonshire Hospital, North-East Front

Clock Tower of the hospital dedicated to Dr W.H. Robertson.

accompanied by the hospital house surgeon but many meetings were held at Buxton, a number at the architect's house in Devonshire Park. By early November 1883 it was the turn of the builder to cross-examine the architect but in the absence of documents, which the architect declined to produce, proceedings were, yet again, postponed. It is not possible to identify precise figures but the sum in dispute may have been as much as £5000.[80] Attempts by Dr W.H. Robertson to persuade the architect to settle at £2,000 were unsuccessful, being a hospital trustee himself R.R. Duke was confident that his side of the case was right and could not agree to the hospital funds being so used.

These protracted negotiations took their toll on both Warburton and Duke, and by now mutterings were being made from various quarters that enough was enough and an offer of a cash settlement to Warburton might get the whole matter cleared up and out of the way. Mr Fox, solicitor, was of the opinion that a figure of £800 might satisfy Warburton, but in the end, after 19 meetings, spanning more than two years, the builder accepted £500 to settle the case.[81] Controversy over the cost of the conversion work and the details of the arbitration issue continued for many years after and the architect, extremely proud of his masterpiece, felt the need to issued a small pamphlet entitled 'Devonshire Hospital, Buxton, 1st October 1902' in which he put forward the facts of the case in exoneration of his decisions as architect.[82]

Provision for Accident Cases

The provision of accident facilities was always a problem for the hospital trustees since, by the nature of its funding and rationale, it existed to treat rheumatic and associated diseases. However, at a meeting of trustees in December 1858 it was agreed to admit accident cases and a new rule appeared in the 1859 Annual Report:

> '...Rule 7. Cases of accident will be admitted to the Hospital on payment of 8s. per week for board and lodging and a guarantee for payment of any extra charges that may be required...'

This may have been prompted by the construction of the Midland Railway into Buxton, taking place at this time, over a spectacular but hazardous route from Rowsley. The chairman of the hospital committee of management was the Burbage industrialist Robert Broome, who had lime and railway interests, and an arrangement was made between the hospital and the Midland Railway Company that the somewhat frequent accident cases should be received at the Devonshire Hospital. The railway company paid the full cost of such cases and the arrangement came to an end after the company opened their station in Buxton in June 1863.

Later arrangements were less formal, however, and did not appear to comply with rule seven. Honorary medical officers referred their accident and surgical cases to the hospital using the subscriber recommendation system to cover the cost. Dr F.K. Dickson, proprietor of Wye House Asylum, sent accident cases arising from his house building investment, Dr R.O.G. Bennet sent cases from the local lime company of which he was surgeon, and both Frederick Turner and W.H. Flint used the same arrangement for their surgical patients. Dr Robertson was opposed to this practice and made his opinion known, but he was in a difficult position because of the honorary work these medical men did for the hospital.[83]

Accident cases continued to be admitted and the conversion of 1879-82 made provision for such referrals in the building attached to the north side of the hospital. This was two-storey, providing such facilities as kitchen, scullery and servants' hall, on the ground floor, and an accident ward and operating room, on the first floor (referred to as the chamber floor), together with inspection wards, nurses room and servants bedrooms. [84]

The Devonshire Hospital continued to provide for accident cases although it is by no means clear that these were always fully paid for by the commercial companies and others who sent patients for treatment. Although some improvement was effected to the accident wards in late 1890, it was becoming clear that, as the town grew and the surrounding limestone industry developed, a greater facility for the treatment of accidents would be needed. In May of 1897, the Chairman of Buxton Urban District Council, E.C. Milligan, held a meeting to consider how provision for accident cases might be developed. This may have led to a decision to improve the facilities at the hospital for in December a sub committee, composed of representatives of the medical staff and others, including the hospital architect, was formed to determine the size and cost of more efficient accommodation and a new operating room.

The architect (now 80 years old) was asked to provide plans for the new accident ward and was authorised to obtain any professional help he needed. He asked one of his former pupils, William Holland, who practised in Buxton, to assist with the designs. R.R. Duke submitted his plans to the sub-committee in May 1898 and later that month a public appeal was launched to finance the building of the accident wards. By August 4th the total received from the public appeal was £1,012 and a tender for the work from John Morten Brown of Bridge Street was accepted at a cost of £1200. The existing accident accommodation was converted to two new Jubilee Accident Wards, named appropriately Victoria and Albert, to accommodate eight patients in total. A tablet over the staircase leading to the unit is carved with the inscription '...*Her Majesty Queen Victoria's Diamond Jubilee 1897 Surgical Wards...*'

A roadway to the new accident ward was laid by Bradshaw and Lowe at a cost of £30 and an application was made to the district council to take over the road after it had been constructed. The rules and regulations governing the admission of accident patients to the new wards were determined by the sub committee in December 1899, a printed set was presented for approval by the hospital management committee at their meeting on 9 February 1900. [85]

The town was fortunate in having an accident unit at the Devonshire Hospital since there appeared to be little enthusiasm by local business and industry to pay for such a facility. Dr Robertson and R.R. Duke had long argued for a separate surgical provision, perhaps a cottage, which could be used as an infirmary and as headquarters for the district nurses and which could be enlarged as demand increased. But the *Buxton Advertiser* had noted in 1898 that there was no probability for some time to come of a surgical hospital being erected in Buxton. [86]

It was clear also that the casualty department at the Devonshire Hospital did not pay for itself, thus it was still supported in part by subscriptions. An analysis kept for the years 1898 to 1904 shows a shortfall every year between payment received and actual cost, some patients were still being paid for through recommendations, though a change in the rules put a stop to this after 1899.[87] The honorary medical officers treated both ordinary and accident patients as did the two salaried house surgeons and the attendants at the accident wards were paid out of the general funds of the Bath Charity.

In 1903 it was decided to keep separate accounts for accident cases, although this was not easy as the management committee saw the accident wards as an integral part of of the hospital and found it practically impossible to charge more than the weekly rate paid by subscribers, which, at the time was 17s. 6d. The committee of management were concerned enough to seek the advice of a

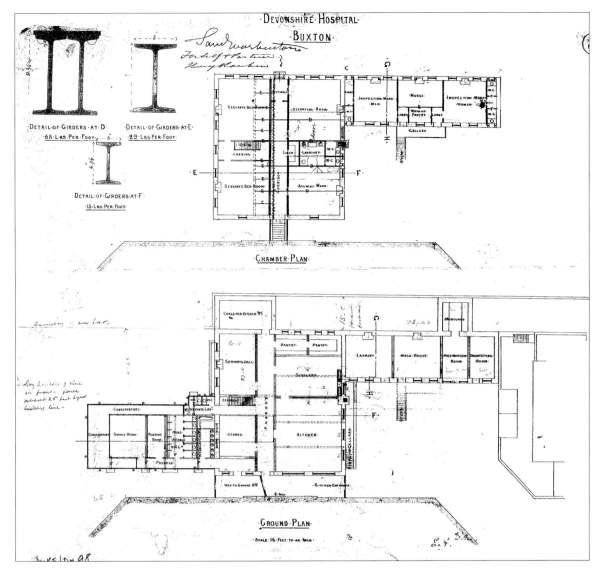

R.R. Duke's working plan no.8 for the 1879-82 conversion shows the accident ward and operating room together with inspection wards, nurses room and servants bedrooms on the first floor above the kitchen, scullery, servants' hall laundry and post-mortem rooms on the ground floor.

legal counsel to determine whether the way in which accident cases were supported breached the rules of the Bath Charity. In 1906 barrister W.O. Danckwerts advised that funds could be used for accident cases, though, eighteen months later in December 1907, his response to a further question was that the committee was not bound indefinitely to keep open and maintain the accident wards but that funds could not legally be paid over to a separate cottage hospital to contribute to accident facilities. [88] It is clear, from annual reports, that the accident provision did remain, although, from 1907, a groundswell of opinion began to urge that a separate provision be made. This resulted in the opening of the Buxton & District Cottage Hospital in 1912.[89]

The accident wards at the Devonshire continued through the First World War treating surgical cases such as bullet and shrapnel wounds but later the buildings were converted to the operating theatre, radiography and pathology departments.

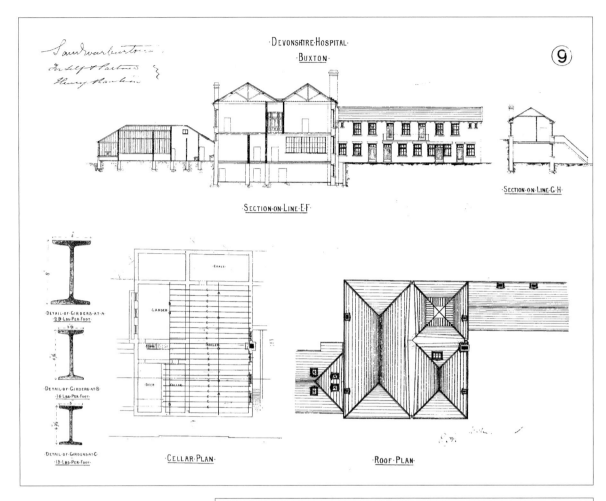

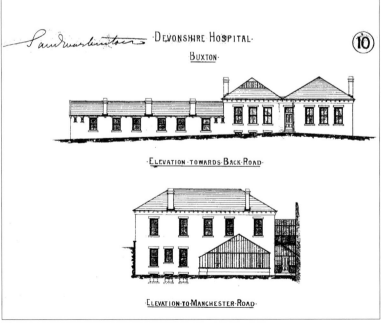

Working plan no. 9 shows the two-storey building of 1879-82 housing the accident provision on the upper floor. The conservatory and smoke room can be seen on the left. The ground-floor rooms on the extreme right were the post-mortem and disinfecting rooms and the mortuary.

The elevations of the building attached to the north side of the hospital housing the accident facilities. The elevation towards the back-road shows that the rising ground behind the hospital was used to advantage to provide an entrance directly into the accident department on the first floor.

The tablet over the internal staircase leading to the Jubilee accident wards.

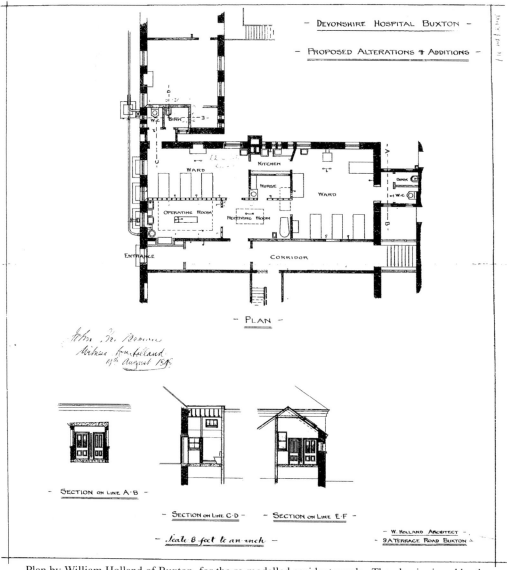

Plan by William Holland of Buxton for the re-modelled accident wards. The plan is signed by the builder John Morten Brown of Bridge Street Buxton and dated 19 August 1898.

Management of the Hospital

The overall direction of the hospital was determined by a Committee of Management which consisted of 14 members drawn from subscribers who lived within a six mile radius of Buxton, five members of the honorary medical staff, the vicar of Buxton, and five persons nominated by the Cotton Districts Convalescent Fund. The chairman of the institution for a particular year was, ex officio, chairman of the management committee, and between 1866 and 1897 this was Dr W.H. Robertson, although after his death the previous tradition of inviting members of the aristocracy to chair was reverted to, for example the Earl of Derby in 1902, the Duke of Portland in 1907 and, naturally, the dukes of Devonshire and other members of the Cavendish family.

The annual meeting, reported in full in the local press, was an opportunity for lavish and refined thanks to be offered to these notables for their patronage and a platform to promote the importance of the hospital nationally.[90] The day-to-day running of the hospital was managed through the House Committee whose membership consisted of the chairman and vice chairman of the management committee plus nine other members. This committee met at least monthly at the hospital and was supported by a secretary and a matron and steward.

The secretary for 36 years, Joseph Taylor, was presented with a silver ink stand on his retirement in 1902, his successor being William Stevenson who already had twenty years service. In 1902, the husband and wife team of matron and steward were replaced when Mr Henry Brailsford retired after the death of his wife, and Mr and Mrs Henry Spalding came from the Liverpool Royal Southern Hospital.

The medical and housekeeping staff needed to run the hospital had more than doubled after the conversion, and in 1870 the secretary and master and matron were supported by thirteen others. By 1888 there was a total of thirty eight staff. Although the specialist medical services were provided by the honorary physicians, by 1888 the hospital was employing two resident house surgeons.[91]

The House Committee was the operational management arm of the hospital and might concern itself with the detail of any aspect of hospital life from extensions and new installations, heating, grounds maintenance to drunken behaviour by patients. The cost of heating was a particular concern, the architect, himself a member of the committee, was often asked to advise on thermal insulation techniques and was to be found calculating usage of coal and coke. For example, in March 1886 a tender was received by the house committee for enclosing the hot water pipes under the floor with brickwork in an attempt to conserve heat loss. The architect proposed that the pipes should instead be covered with felt and old carpeting throughout the whole length which was done and he also spoke to the engineer and steward to explain how better heating economy might be achieved by attention and care.[92]

At the December 1889 meeting, the hospital steward was requested to report the amount of coal and coke used monthly at the hospital and at the hospital baths; also to report on the amount of butcher's meat consumed and the quantity of gas used for lighting and cooking. It was requested that the Matron should report monthly on the number of articles washed in the hospital laundry and that the house surgeon submit an inventory of goods in the dispensary with detailed stock accounts of drugs and medicines, also that he report monthly to the committee the results of the weekly milk testing.[93] A later note to members shows how savings were made in food. In October 1903 Henry Spalding submitted a comparison of four items, butchers' meat, butter, tea and beer, showing the considerable savings he had made in the previous nine months. No doubt this was an early indication to the committee of his housekeeping ability. [94]

In their endeavours the committee were kept on their toes by fairly frequent comparisons of costs between their undertaking and others. In January of 1883 the Duke of Devonshire's resident agent, Frank Drewry, raised with the architect the high cost of keeping patients suggesting that the committee investigate reducing costs materially and intimating that the interest taken by the duke extended to the quality of its management. A year later the governors of the CDCF raised the comparison between the hospital and the Southport Convalescent Home suggesting that Buxton's costs were a third higher. Whilst such challenges might be countered on the basis of not comparing like with like, they may have provided the incentive for more detailed inspections of hospital operations. In July 1888 one of the management committee, John Baker JP, supported by Mr G. Wainwright, a CDCF representative, proposed

'*...That the committee appoint a sub-committee to investigate and enquire into the general management of the hospital, and to consider the rules and regulations of the same and report to the committee of management the result of such an enquiry and to suggest any alterations in the management or rules that they might deem necessary. In doing this they should have free access to all books, minutes, accounts and contracts connected with the hospital they require and that the officials and servants of the hospital render them every assistance and give them all the information they may demand. Such a sub-committee would consist of not less than three and not more than five members...*' [95]

Precisely why there should be a lack of confidence amongst some members of the board of management is not known, but despite objections from the chairman, on the grounds that the records of the board could be examined privately at any time without the need for any formal enquiry, the board voted on the proposal, the motion was passed and the sub-committee was formed. Mr J. Baker, was asked to nominate the members of the sub-committee and he selected four members including the architect. The Chairman of the trustees, Dr Robertson, was invited to be an ex-officio member. J.W. Taylor, a prominent Buxton solicitor, declined to take his place on the grounds that the CDCF was not sufficiently well represented by only having one member on the committee.

This was a lengthy inquiry, and the findings did not reach the board of management until 7 December 1889 when Mr Baker wished to have thirty copies of the report made up and distributed amongst the trustees and governors. However, an amendment was carried that a special meeting of the committee of management should be called to consider the report before sending it to be printed and this meeting was organised for 21 December 1889. This was a contentious report which made some critical observations on the management style of the hospital. Mr J.W. Taylor objected to his name being

Joseph Taylor who was secretary to the hospital during the major conversion and retired in 1902 after 36 years service.

included on the report as he had declined to serve on the committee from the outset and his name was duly removed. R.R. Duke made clear certain parts of the report with which he disagreed. It was thought by the committee of management that a general publication of the sub-committees findings could damage the reputation of the hospital, in particular that it might affect subscriber confidence, and it was decided to take up the offer of Mr Mclure (CDCF governor) to have twenty-five confidential copies of the report written up at his office so that every member of the committee might have a copy.

No copy of the report has come to light but it can be inferred that the criticisms levelled at the committee were largely to do with excessive expenditure and suggestions were put forward to make changes in the rules and the manner in which the hospital was managed. Mr Baker was far from happy with the outcome of the committee's findings and moved that a copy of the report should be sent to every subscriber of the hospital within a six mile radius, but it seemed that the committee of management was gradually distancing itself from Mr Baker's stance and his motion was not seconded. Mr Baker also requested that a further special meeting of the board be called to consider the report and suggestions of rule changes were made, but the majority decision of the Board was that the matter need go no further and should be laid to rest. Mr Baker continued to insist that the report should receive the attention that he thought was due to it and gave notice that on Saturday June 7th he would move that certain rules be rescinded and that others, a copy of which he had circulated to every member of the committee, be adopted instead. As promised, Mr Baker moved his proposal, but it was not seconded and the affair was at an end. This episode shows that the management of the hospital was prepared to examine its own effectiveness, but only up to a point, and the manner in which longer established trustees closed ranks on John Baker, a relative newcomer, is perhaps indicative of their resistance to more modern management methods at the time. [96]

Ten years later, a detailed inspection of the hospital was undertaken by Dr F.K. Dickson and Mr H.A. Hubbersty, who presented their findings to colleagues on the management committee in September 1899. The observations on hospital cleanliness, decoration, sanitary arrangements, water closets and patient washing arrangements, amongst others, were direct and hard-hitting. They were challenged by the architect in a printed reply in December, in a somewhat selective and defensive manner, but they led to a subsequent extension programme in 1900 which included replacement of sanitary fittings. [97]

Other committees were formed for particular purposes; the work of the Building Sub-Committee in supervising the hospital conversion has been described. An important sub-committee was formed following the hospital conversion and protracted arbitration. It met on June 6th 1884 to consider the account submitted by the architect for his professional charges for this work. His total fee was £1546 of which he had received £1200 account leaving a balance of £346 which the committee disputed. It is possible that members were wary of the increased costs of the conversion for which they held the architect, in part, responsible. The architect met with the sub-committee to explain in detail how his fees were calculated and to impress upon members his genuine attempts to be prudent and after some further discussion the figure of £300 was mutually agreed and settled.

In 1888 a sub-committee examined the plumbing work required in the hospital concluding that a full-time plumber and painter should be engaged.

Subscribers and 'Recommends'

The earnestness with which members of the management committee set about their task reflects the sedulous interest they showed in the patients. The method of financing the hospital had not changed from the original conception of 'subscribers' and 'recommends' found in the early rules of the Buxton Bath Charity, but the rules were modified over time. Thus by the start of the First World War the rules allowed for a life subscription of 20 guineas where the subscriber could recommend one in-patient and two out-patients annually. An annual subscriber could recommend one in-patient or four out-patients for each guinea annually subscribed. It was also possible to pay a casual subscription of £2.12s.6d to recommend one in-patient and there were a number of other incentives for subscribers to recommend additional patients. Clergymen preaching sermons which raised more than £3 in a year and proprietors of hotels, hydros and lodging houses who raised more than £5 per year, were also entitled to recommend one in-patient or four out-patients. The term 'recommend' in reality meant admission since the management committee would not turn down a patient whose disease was capable of being benefited by the Buxton Waters. Such diseases included forms of rheumatism, gout and arthritis and those illnesses listed in the appendix, but certain cases were excluded:

> '...*Persons suffering from any incurable or Infectious Disorder or from advanced Heart Disease - women more than six months advanced in Pregnancy - persons in the later stages of consumption - or afflicted with Fits, Cutaneous Disease, Ulcers, Itch or Insanity - or infested with vermin cannot be admitted as in-patients; or, if inadvertently admitted, cannot be allowed to remain...*' [98]

These 'recommends' were very much part of the social cache of the Buxton 'polite society' and they were borrowed and repaid on a regular basis. On 20 June 1896 Mrs Sibilla Pettit wrote from Holm Leigh School to Mrs Aston Smith:

> '...*Dear Mrs Smith, We are going to have the boys' sports on Saturday July 4th on the Park ground and I shall be very pleased if you will all come and see them at 2.30. Have you a hospital ticket to spare? I have given mine away and my daughter, Mrs Moxon wants one very much for a young woman in her parish. The doctors say it would prevent her rheumatism from becoming chronic...*
>
> *With kindest regards, Believe me to be yours very sincerely...*' [99]

On 8 October 1898, Mrs Florence Little, wife of the Head of Buxton College, wrote a postcard to a friend

> '...*I should feel much obliged if you could let me know if Mr Duke has a recommend for the hospital and if so do you think he would bestow it on me! I had a letter from a friend of ours this morning - a clergyman in Southport - who wants one for a poor old woman, a parishioner of his... I am very sincerely yours...*' [100]

Most subscribers paid one or two guineas, some paid five, but others were more generous, for example in 1900 and 1901, Jesse Boot, the founder of the Boots Pure Drug Company in Nottingham, subscribed £10.10s.0d. By 1914 Sir Jesse had reduced this to £5.5s.0d. In that same year, amongst more than 1200 subscribers, the Duke of Norfolk gave £26.5s.0d, and an anonymous 'L.R.' (probably a member of the wealthy Rothschild family) donated £10.10s.0d. Commercial companies also subscribed, for example, Brunner Mond (forerunner of Imperial Chemical Industries)

£10.10s.0d., the Butterley Iron Company of Ripley, £15.15s.0. and the Midland Railway, £10.10s.0d.

More than 600 societies subscribed including many Hospital Funds and Co-operative Societies throughout the country. Further funds were raised by collections after sermons in various churches, and in Buxton these were held on a 'Hospital Sunday'. In 1890 a determined effort was made to introduce a 'Hospital Saturday' when large collecting boxes were placed around the town, though donation boxes were kept in some hotels, shops and other public places all the year round. The charity was supported by other donations and bequests, some of which were recorded on a board hung in the dome of the hospital. These were from £20 upwards and included a regular proportion of the money obtained from admissions to the Duke of Devonshire's Chatsworth House. In addition to money, all manner of gifts were made, ranging from rabbits to cheese, and to pyjamas and warm clothes. A separate arrangement was made to assist patients with the cost of travelling to and from the hospital. Known as the 'Samaritan Fund' the money came from a number of individual and commercial legacies and endowments invested to provide an income for the purpose and to support poor people who were unable to obtain a recommendation. [101]

Patients

The hospital could accommodate just under 300 patients in eight wards for women, eight for men and two surgical. In 1899 the architect calculated 128 beds for women, 160 for men and eight surgical beds.[102] Patients were drawn from across England, an analysis of the annual report for 1898 shows patients coming from more than 450 locations, but many of the largest numbers were from the north of England, for example, Bolton (60), Burnley (25), Derby (105), Leeds (53), Liverpool (64), Manchester and Salford (293), Sheffield (168), Rochdale (48) and Stockport (35), although 112 patients came from London in that year.

Over 130 different occupations are described, the largest categories being carters & dray men (41), colliers & miners (208), cotton operatives - male (66), female (68), domestic duties (chiefly married women) (739), weavers (97), gardeners (62) and labourers (381).

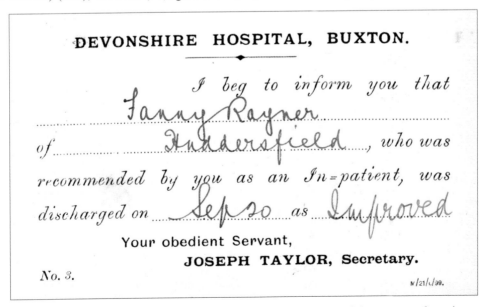

Postcard dated 20 September 1899 sent to a subscriber giving details of the progress of a patient.

Most patients were suffering from some form of rheumatic disease which was described as disease of the locomotor system. Of the total of 2947 cases, 2356 fell into this category. Other categories included diseases of the nervous system (322 cases), respiratory (17) and debility (44). Those suffering from diseases involving more than one system numbered 113 cases and the surgical department's 19 cases included sprained ankle, head wound, circular saw accident, blasting accident and the amputation of a crushed foot. [103]

It will be seen that the largest category was 'domestic duties (chiefly married women)' and an analysis shows this to be the case through the annual reports of the later 19th century. This suggests that particular female problems were treatable at the Buxton Baths, indeed may have been something of a specialism. Dr Robertson refers to treating '.....*much of the deranged health incidental to middle-age in females - much of the uterine irregularity and disturbed condition incidental to females at various periods of life...*' and Dr Samuel Hyde identifies a category of '*diseases of women*' where he specifies particular illnesses. However, it has been pointed out that, by today's standards, it is likely that women were more generally under-represented in the hospital, at between thirty and thirty-five percent of the patient total, given that it is now known that three times the number of women suffer from rheumatoid arthritis than men.[104] An analysis for the year 1914 giving more details of all patients treated is in the appendix.

Patients were seen by the physician and after diagnosis were prescribed medication and or mineral water baths, either at the natural temperature of 82° F., or at higher temperatures in the Hot Baths. The hospital measured its success by the numbers of patients who after three weeks of treatment (or longer in some cases) could be described as 'cured' or 'relieved', although the term 'improved' was sometimes used. After treatment a postcard was sent to each subscriber who had recommended a patient, indicating the date of discharge and their medical condition. The well-being of patients was assessed on a regular basis by House Visitors who would walk the wards and speak to patients before making any comments in a report book. In 1900 the House Visitors included such notables as Mr A.W.Slack, solicitor, Mr Otto Hoffman, an exporter, Mr and Mrs Jesse Boot, Boots Pure Drug Co., Mrs Robert Parker, wife of a bank manager, Mrs John Cumming Bates, widow of the founder of *Buxton Advertiser*, and Mrs Charles Heathcote, wife of a prominent architect.

There is no doubt that medical benefit was obtained by patients using the baths and water treatments, but, for many, three weeks at Buxton was also a blessed relief from a hazardous or dirty or just plain monotonous occupation. The rest and recuperation was of benefit to most patients, but the discipline and routine of the hospital was always a first consideration, even at Christmas, as may be seen from this report in the *Buxton Advertiser* for 1 January 1903

'...*The Christmas festival at the Devonshire Hospital was ushered in by the domestic staff singing carols at 5 o'clock in the morning. At 8 o'clock breakfast was served to the patients and each was the recipient of a present. Dinner consisted of roast beef, plum pudding and mince pies, and afterwards there was dessert. The dining-hall was well filled for the Christmas banquet and after dinner songs were sung and games indulged in. Tea was served at 5 o'clock and a little later an excellent entertainment was given, consisting of songs, recitations and piano solos...*' [105]

Doctors and Medical Staff

The honorary medical officers were drawn from the elite of the water medical specialists in town. Foremost amongst them was the long serving chairman of the hospital trustees, W.H. Robertson (1810-1897). Robertson came to Buxton in 1835, after graduating MD at Edinburgh, and began to develop what was to become a formidable reputation in the treatment of cases of a 'rheumatic and gouty nature'. In 1837 he was appointed Honorary Physician to the Devonshire Hospital. By 1888 Dr Robertson had been an acting physician of the Devonshire Hospital for fifty years and to commemorate the occasion he was presented with a life sized portrait of himself painted by Mr J.H.E. Partington of Stockport. Dr Robertson's wife was presented with a smaller version of the portrait. The portrait, mounted in a massive gilt frame, was later hung in the hospital boardroom.

Robertson was chairman of the committee of management for thirty one years until his death in 1897 and he was undoubtedly the most influential medical doctor in town during its most important period of growth as an inland medical resort. He did much to promote the unique properties of the Buxton thermal water, eschewing the hydropathic fashion of his time and staying firmly in the mainstream of medical reputation and the techniques of hydrotherapy.

There is a distinct difference between the terms hydropathy and hydrotherapy as applied in Robertson's time. Hydropathy referred to a method of cold water treatment popularised by Vincent Priessnitz (1799-1851) in Austrian Silesia. His method did not rely upon the properties of a natural mineral water, any cold water would do, the important thing was the way in which the water was applied coupled with a regime of diet and exercise in good, preferably mountain, air. The approach was promoted in England by a Captain R.T. Claridge who described the treatment in detail in a book published in 1842. The fashion took off, hydropathic centres were established in many parts of the country, and doctors specialising in this form of treatment began to make a name for themselves. Thus the hydropathic hotel emerged where clients could stay, often in some degree of comfort, to take a particular 'water cure' which was not of itself particularly comfortable and might include wrapping in wet sheets to induce sweating, being sprayed from a considerable height with water onto an affected joint or sitting half-immersed in a bath and receiving a douche or water spray. Some centres with a natural mineral water developed a reputation for hydropathy and associated hydropathics, Buxton's nearest neighbour Matlock was one; another, Malvern was visited by notable literary and scientific figures such as Charles Darwin, Alfred Tennyson and Thomas Carlyle; and in the north of England, Ben Rhydding, Ilkley offered more innovatory treatment including a compressed air bath. This hydropathic fashion caused great debate amongst the established medical practitioners and stimulated many column inches in journals such as The Lancet. The method was likened to other 'quack' medicines available at the time such as, mesmerism and mesmero-phrenology and considered both dangerous and ineffective medically.

Dr Robertson was firmly inside the established medical school and this is why Buxton was not in the forefront of this movement, a medical water centre needed a mineral water with special properties. It is notable that two other medical resorts at least did not move rapidly to embrace hydropathy either, Buxton's northern rival Harrogate and Bath in Somerset. Towards the end of the century the huge range of treatments came together to form the science of 'balneology' which included all forms of water treatment, electro-hydro, massage and other therapies, as well as climate and diet as the sanatorium movement also developed.

Dr William Henry Robertson was a most influential man in town, perhaps the most important figure after the Duke of Devonshire's agent, and he did much to promote the reputation of Buxton mineral water and the work of the Devonshire Hospital nationally. His *Buxton Guide* ran to eleven editions and his smaller *Guide to the use of the Buxton Waters* continued after his death in 1897 with the 27th edition, edited by Dr George Lorimer, in 1898. He also contributed papers to *The Lancet*. The whole town mourned Robertson's death; his cortege, accompanied by many notable townspeople, passing shops closed and shuttered and flags at half mast, as it moved from 6, The Square, his home for forty years, to St John's Church. [106]

Robertson was supported by a number of other doctors who advanced their reputation at Buxton. Accepting a position of honorary physician to the Devonshire Hospital was not entirely philanthropic; true the doctors gave their services free but this was not a demanding requirement, indeed it probably offered the inquiring medic opportunities to experiment with treatment or follow up particular ideas. It was also something of an honour to be invited to the post and such doctors, in support of their private practice, could, and did cite Devonshire Hospital patients as case-studies of their success.

In the period 1883 to 1914, thirteen other doctors are recorded as giving their services to the hospital. The Shipton dynasty produced several doctors in Buxton beginning with William Parker Shipton (1818-1895) who was a member of the medical staff of the Buxton Bath Charity from 1852 and became consulting surgeon in 1860. He came to Buxton in about 1852 and developed a thriving practice from 2 The Square, where he lived for nearly forty years. Shipton had three sons, two of whom followed him into medicine (the third went into law). Arthur Shipton (1856-1937) became honorary physician in 1879 and an honorary consultant in 1901; his brother, Herbert Shipton (1865-1925), became honorary physician from 1902. The Shiptons were keen cricketers and played for the Buxton team, Herbert, being a particularly useful slow bowler, who appeared in 2nd class county matches. In recounting the life of the elder Shipton, William Parker, the obituary writer, excelled in demonstrating the esteem with which the man, and his family, were held in town:

'...*He was a regular attend at St John's church where his fine face lent additional reverence and dignity to the south transept...*'

Dr John Braithwaite (1871-1940) was in practice in Buxton at Norman House, Hardwick Mount for sixteen years and became a honorary consulting physician in 1902. He was captain of the Buxton and High Peak Golf Club and also played cricket. In 1914 he volunteered to work with the French Red Cross where he was twice mentioned in dispatches and awarded the DSO and the Croix de Guerre with palm. His second wife was Margaret, daughter of Dr Arthur Shipton.

Dr Robert Ottiwell Gifford Bennet (1832-1902) was an honorary physician for forty two years from 1860. He lived at Tankerville House in Hardwick Street and later at Park Place, Buxton, and he also built the mansion Bennetstone Hall at Barmoor Clough near Chapel-en-le-Frith. He was a wealthy man, son of a Manchester attorney, and he invested considerably in working-class houses in the town notably in Bennet Street and Hogshaw. He published *Buxton and its Medicinal Waters*, a small book which ran to three known editions.

Frederick Turner MRCS, LSA (1843-1914) became an honorary physician in 1865. He was the son of Samuel Turner, a townsman influential in Buxton's early urban growth. Frederick Turner had a career in public health becoming Medical Officer of the Buxton District of the Chapel-en-le-Frith Union and, subsequently Medical Officer of Health for the Buxton Urban District. His expertise in the sanitary standards and community health was of great benefit to the Devonshire Hospital.

Francis Kennedy Dickson (1843-1907) followed his father, Thomas, as proprietor of the Wye House Asylum in Buxton, an establishment for the care and treatment of mentally ill patients of the middle and upper classes. He held the post of honorary acting medical officer from 1865 and was appointed honorary consulting physician in 1878. He also served on the management committee and was very involved in the running of the hospital and in new developments such as the Jubilee accident wards. He supported the Buxton and District Nursing Fund which helped to finance nursing staff at the hospital.

Dr Albert Octavius Haslewood (b.1844) was an honorary medical officer from 1886 and a honorary consultant in 1906, he was also a member of the management committee. Dr Haslewood's practice was at 11 Terrace Road.

George Lorimer MD (1846-1908) began his association with the hospital as a residential house surgeon from 1873-1884 becoming honorary physician in 1902. He wrote *Health Resorts - Buxton* in 1906 and edited Dr Robertson's *A Guide to the use of Buxton Waters* from 1898. He lived and practised from 9 Terrace Road, Buxton.

Dr Thomas Buxton Flint (b. 1869) practised from 22 Hardwick Street and was a honorary medical officer from 1902. He was also the medical officer at the Buxton Urban District sanatorium on Bakewell Road and the certifying factory surgeon for the Buxton district. He later became a J.P.

Dr Charles W. Buckley (d.1955), who became an honorary physician to the hospital in 1912, lived initially in Robertson Road but, from 1906, practised in Hardwick Terrace next door to Dr John Braithwaite. He was active in local politics becoming the mayor of Buxton in 1924 and later moved to 5, The Square.

Dr Frank Reginald Sawdon was medical officer and public vaccinator for the Buxton District of the Chapel-en-le-Frith Union and had his practice at 3 Hardwick street. He became an honorary physician to the hospital in 1913.

Dr George Hobson Thompson (b.1858) became an honorary medical officer in 1907 and a honorary consultant in 1912. He practised from 1 High Street in Higher Buxton. In 1903 he was a vice president of the Society of Climatology and Balneology, a professional group concerned with all aspects of water and related medicine. Other doctors in town were members of this society.

Once elected to the honorary position these doctors would generally serve until retirement or death and many of them produced an impressive length of tenure. They were supported by other honorary posts, including dentists, a meteorologist and, as techniques developed, a consulting electrical engineer for electro-water treatment, and masseur and masseuse. All these complemented the full-time staff which grew through the century to include a house surgeon and assistant house surgeon, a clinical pathologist, in charge of the bacteriological laboratory, and a pharmaceutical dispenser.

The matron and house steward provided resident supervision. These medical staff saw the town of Buxton grow in reputation as an inland medical and pleasure resort in the period between 1882 and the start of the First World War, and it was clear the hospital could not stand still during this time. Medical techniques were moving on, electricity was being applied in treatments, procedures in massage were developing, treatments using Röentgen rays (x-rays), and radiant heat and light-cure methods, were coming in to use. The management committee were busy with a constant updating of the hospital facilities as well as maintenance work.

LEFT: Dr William Henry Robertson (1810-1897) Honorary Physician to the Buxton Bath Charity from 1837 and chairman of the committee of management of the Devonshire Hospital for thirty one years until his death in 1897. He was most influential in shaping and directing the Hospital through its most important phases of growth.

Dr Francis Kennedy Dickson (1843-1907) proprietor of the Wye House Asylum in Buxton, an establishment for the care and treatment of mentally ill patients of the middle and upper classes. He was honorary acting medical officer of the Devonshire Hospital from 1865 and appointed honorary consulting physician in 1878. He also served on the management committee and was very involved in the running of the hospital and in new developments such as the Jubilee accident wards.

Frederick Turner MRCS, LSA (1843-1914) became an honorary physician in 1865. He had a career in public health becoming Medical Officer of the Buxton District of the Chapel-en-le-Frith Union and, subsequently Medical Officer of Health for the Buxton Urban District. His expertise in the sanitary standards and community health was of great benefit to the Devonshire Hospital.

Dr Charles W. Buckley (d.1955) became an honorary physician to the hospital in 1912. From 1906 he practised in Hardwick Terrace. He was active in local politics, the mayor of Buxton in 1924 and is shown here in his mayoral robes

Refurbishment and Improvement

Soon after the major conversion further work was needed on the drainage system. This was instigated by Dr Frederick Turner, Medical Officer of Health, who wrote to Dr Robertson in 1884 expressing his concern about the admission of sewer gas into the official apartments of the hospital and asking if there had been any recorded cases of typhoid or other febrile disease. The architect described to the committee an old main from where, he conjectured, sewer gas was escaping. The town surveyor, Joseph Hague, was called in and he submitted plans for a complete re-drainage to the hospital for an estimated cost of about £375. Furthermore the drains would need to be re-laid and an outlay of about £150 would be necessary to correct the closets and lavatories. An additional £150 would be needed to construct an efficient ventilation system to the lavatories. He also recommended the laying of a bed of concrete underneath the floor of the dome and extension making a total cost of £835. Mr Hague attended a meeting of the hospital house committee in February 1885 and explained that the new Bostel's Patent Closet had been chosen for installation and, as Mr Bostel himself was visiting the hospital soon, he would explain the benefits of his closets. Tenders were sought and the firm of Pindard and Gill installed twenty-five Bostel's closets by July, the remaining contract being completed by the end of December 1885. [107]

Ventilation remained a continuing problem in the hospital with complaints from the house surgeon concerning wards and the consulting room, resulting in some additional 'Tobin' ventilation tubes being ordered in 1893. Two years later the architect was asked to report on the ventilation situation, amongst other things, and a sub-committee of the house committee was set up to consider his report. This was composed of Dr Bennet, Dr Dickson, Mr F Drewry and the architect and, after inspecting different parts of the hospital, the members agreed to changes in the layout of windows, installation of more Tobin ventilation tubes and the provision of openings in the outer walls of the large dormitories and in the floors between the hot water coils to overcome the problems. Other work included the provision of a bath for the nurses and the dividing up of number seven ward and three smaller wards to be re-used as a library, lavatories and the lift room. Plans for these works were drawn up by the architect and the work was carried out by Mr E. Brown, a local builder for £22.

The sub-committee also considered the question of installing a lift in order that the first floor wards might be used for less ambulant patients. Tenders were obtained from eight firms and the architect recommended Messrs Archibald Smith and Stevens of London and Manchester as the most suitable. The firm's representative, Mr C.C.Major, was invited to a meeting of the sub-committee on 17 September 1896 to describe, and answer questions on, his firm's product. Mr Major was questioned in detail by the architect who, whilst not opposed to the installation of a lift, was very concerned about the safety aspects. He asked many technical questions such as, details of cable breaking strains and the systems that would come into operation in the case of cable failure. The lift in question worked on a counterbalance principle and was operated from the inside by a pull-rope. It was designed to hold a patient in bed and two helpers at the sides, although allowance was made for the lift to take at least twice that weight. Mr Major agreed to supply and fit the lift for the sum of £75 and to supply 'Borthwick' collapsible gates charged by the foot length. The lift was guaranteed for one year and annual inspections would be carried out by his firm at the cost of £1.1s.0d. [108]

The grounds of the hospital were considered a valuable recreational resource for patients and in December of 1886 it was resolved to again ask Mr Adam Hogg, the curator of the hugely popular

Pavilion Gardens, to put the hospital grounds into good order. Ironically, earlier that year the separate conservatory and smoking room had been opened out into one room to provide a larger area for smokers when the hospital was full! In a report of the hospital and Bath Charity in July of 1891 Dr Robertson, referring to the hospital dome, said that the value of the half acre covered, warmed and ventilated interior circle of the hospital for the exercise and recreation of the patients could not be too highly estimated. But this facility required quite expensive maintenance. In 1890 the builder Edward Brown of Bridge Street repaired the floor by cutting away spaces at intervals under the hot water pipes to allow ventilation. Another local builder, G.J. Bagshaw, had declined to do the work unless the whole floor was taken up and relaid. In 1892 the whole floor was thoroughly cleaned and saturated with raw and boiled linseed oil.[109] In 1899 the dome was repainted for the first time since its erection, the ironwork in bright tints of blue, chocolate and white, with the ceiling distempered in white. The Manchester firm of Messrs Horsfield and Son carried out the work at a cost of £300.[110]

A noted feature of the dome is its acoustics; standing directly under the centre it is possible to experience a perfect dropping echo, and conversation between two people at the circumference is not easy because the sound travels diametrically across to the other side of the dome. The earliest discussions on deadening the echo took place at a meeting of the house committee in January 1889 when it was planned to use the dome for fund-raising hospital concerts. The idea put forward was to have a sounding board fixed over the platform, but, in order to test this before entailing expense and changing the structural appearance, a canvas sheet was stretched across the ironwork below the lantern. It proved unsatisfactory and no evidence of any subsequent successful attempts have come to light. It is interesting to note that the famous Albert Hall in London had similar problems and these were mainly solved by sounding arrangements in the space of the dome above the performing area.

Arising from an inspection report by Dr F.K. Dickson and Mr H.A. Hubbersty in 1899, hospital improvements were proposed at a meeting, in June 1900, of a sub-committee responsible for fabric, sanitation and building. It was decided to extend the lavatory buildings and change the layout to increase the number of wash basins and WCs on the ground and chamber floors of both the mens' and womens' areas of the hospital. According to the architect's notes, this entailed the installation of 39 new water-closets, sixty wash basins and two slop sinks which were obtained from Shanks of Stoke on Trent at a cost of £340. The work was spread over a year with the new buildings by Messrs Wild and the plumbing by the local firm of Edwin Broomhead & Sons of Market Place. The extensions also included the installation of ventilation shafts to the laundry, repairs to the roof and the installation of a new hot water boiler. The work was completed in May 1901 and the total cost was £2,183.[111]

Whilst the architect to the hospital, R.R. Duke, who was also a trustee, kept his hand on any building plans right up to his death, in 1909, some work was carried out by the architect William Radford Bryden, who purchased Duke's architectural practice in 1883. Bryden drew plans for work at the hospital Hot Baths which included alterations to the roof and floor in 1887/8, though his major work was the provision of the new baths at the hospital in 1914 which are described in chapter four. Other work at the hospital baths in George Street included a replacement steam pump fitted in 1894 and a new pump to supply the drinking fountain and steam pump boiler in 1896. R.R. Duke provided a number of additional embellishments to the central area of the hospital as gifts. In 1895 he donated oak panels which were fitted on either side of the main entrance. It was his original intention to have the panels painted with sketches representing the 'troubling' of the waters (the natural movements within the emerging spring water mixed with the gases). However, he was unable to find suitable illustrations for the purpose and decided to use extracts from two sermons which had been given by the late Bishop of Manchester on a visit to the hospital. The Bishop had said that he had seen the troubling of the Buxton Waters, that clear blue fluid in the bath, troubled, moved into eddies and whirls by the gas which came up from the bowels of the earth. It was God's way of troubling these waters and making them answer to the healing purpose. Buxton had this gift, he called it a gift, from God. On the opposite side of the entrance were the words:

> '...This hospital was established in the year 1859 for the relief of the poor persons from all parts of Great Britain and Ireland, suffering from rheumatism, gout etc. who otherwise could not avail themselves of the benefit of the use of the celebrated thermal waters...'

and over the entrance arch, painted in large lettering, '...Freely ye have received, freely give...'

The architect was himself chairman of the trustees and committee of management from September 1900, due to the death of Mr Henry Shaw, and, although he was most proud of this elevation, he held the position only until the January meeting of 1901 when he personally moved that the 8th Duke of Devonshire be elected chairman for the forthcoming year. In the year of his chairmanship the architect arranged for an oak frame containing a portrait of the 7th Duke of Devonshire to be cleaned and regilded and for the ducal coronet and Cavendish motto, 'Cavendo Tutus' to be painted by Mrs Laura Shaw, an accomplished amateur artist. Mrs Shaw presented this to the hospital in memory of her late husband and it remains today hung in the dome.

In November 1901 a plaster model of a statue of the seventh Duke of Devonshire was set into the middle of the dome floor. The statue, which had been used to cast the bronze statue of the duke in Eastbourne, had been donated by the sculptor, Mr W Gascombe-Johns from his studio in St John's Wood, NW1. It was seven feet tall and was transported to Buxton by train to the Midland Railway station on 26 November. The model was mounted on a wooden pedestal of five feet in height and the floorboards were cut away in the centre of the dome to enable a brick base to provide a firm foundation. A number of contemporary photographs exist but the statue itself was moved shortly after the hospital became managed by the National Health Service in 1948, and has not survived.

Visitors of all Ranks

Dr Robertson, frequently described, in glowing terms, the architectural uniqueness of the Devonshire Hospital, its loftiness and its likeness to the 'pavilion' principle of hospital construction, and it is certainly true that the building became a tourist attraction as soon as the domed roof was completed. As early as July 1883 the management committee resolved that visitors should be allowed to ascend the dome for a charge of 6d per person and that notice-boards to this effect be placed in the entrance. It is assumed that those ascending would have climbed the curved metal ladder which is fixed to the outside of the dome, a feat requiring a steady head and no fear of heights! It is not known how many rose to this challenge but the hospital was visited by many people each day who came to view and, no doubt, experience the perfect echo in the centre of the dome. The architect kept some figures in his notebook showing a total of 5,546 between 4 August and 14 October 1902, a surprising number in two and a half months. Visitors to this day marvel at the construction of the dome roof and, before the building finally closed as a hospital, many went home with a copy of the hospital guide book. The inscription around the inside of the colonnade reads:

'...One half of this building was given to the use of the sick poor by William Spencer Cavendish sixth Duke of Devonshire in the year 1859 and conveyed to the trustees as the Devonshire Hospital together with the pleasure grounds by William Cavendish, seventh Duke of Devonshire, in the year 1868. The remainder of the building was obtained in the year 1878 and the whole was internally reconstructed by the Governors of the Cotton Districts Convalescent Fund in the year 1881...'

In 1882 the trustees had been unable to secure a visit by the Prince of Wales to open the newly converted hospital, but more than twenty years later, on 7 January 1905, he came as King Edward VII, with his queen, Alexandra. The royal party drove directly to the Devonshire Hospital through a town whose streets were lined with people and completely decorated with flags, bunting and messages of welcome and loyalty. They toured the hospital and spoke to patients and staff, visiting the Jubilee Accident Wards and the operating theatre, and both were most impressed with the hospital's work. The King expressed particular interest in the echo of the dome suggesting that it was not quite as effective as that of the Baptistery at Pisa but still a wonderful echo. Both the King and Queen met the hospital architect, by now 88 years old and in a wheelchair. The party, which included the Duke and Duchess of Devonshire, was conducted around the hospital by the senior medical man Dr Frederick Turner. Later, over lunch at the St Ann's Hotel, the king offered Dr Turner a new glass operating table to replace the wooden one he had seen on his tour. [112] The operating table which arrived was, however, made of copper and brass and was, for some time, on display in the Devonshire Hospital dome; it is now displayed at Stepping Hill Hospital, Stockport.

The royal party outside the Devonshire Hospital during the visit of King Edward VII
and Queen Alexandra in January 1905.

Optimism in Town and Hospital before the Great War

The visit of the King and Queen came at a time when the resort of Buxton was at the height of its popularity, the town buoyant, the future looked bright and the Devonshire Hospital an important asset in the developing medical reputation. The hospital was showing a positive balance sheet and had more than £22,000 in investments to support further developments. The period to 1914 saw further growth of facilities at the hospital. The private houses, 'Northleigh Villas', adjacent to the outside lodge of the hospital, previously owned by the Buxton draper and hospital trustee, Edward Chambers Milligan, were purchased by the hospital in 1907 for £2,478 and 1 Northleigh was progressively converted and furnished in 1908 and 1913 to provide a nurses' home.[113] In more recent times the house was occupied by the hospital secretary. The other half of the building, referred to as No.2 Northleigh in 1933, had been renamed 'Wyndholme' by 1939. Between 1947 and 1951 Dr C.W. Buckley rented consulting rooms there after which it was used as residential accommodation for the physician and the matron. [114]

'Chiswick House', at the rear of the hospital on Marlborough Road, formerly owned by Mr Joseph Webster, was bought by the charity in 1913 at a cost, including alterations for hospital use, of £4,156. In the same year a small amount was spent on the furnishing of wards in the hospital. The final payment for the installation of electric lighting to the hospital was made in 1914. In July 1909 the hospital architect attended his last meeting of the management committee in a wheelchair and met the 9th Duke of Devonshire, so that he could then say he had met four dukes of Devonshire during his lifetime. Robert Rippon Duke died in August 1909 at the age of 92 years, having been connected with the Devonshire Hospital as trustee and architect for fifty years and having seen the building transformed from stables to busy hospital - a remarkable career.

In all that time, however, the architect had not seen the hospital acquire its own mineral water baths on site, despite attempts by himself and others to bring this about. Though valuable strides in medical development and hospital facilities had been won in the 30 years from the time of the hospital conversion, patients were still required to walk down a steep road to George Street and the Square to take the water treatment. Furthermore the patient had to return up the hill to the hospital on foot after treatment, at a time when the body was relaxed and the pores of the skin open. Of course those unable to walk were wheeled down but most, it seems, walked. It was time for the hospital to offer its range of medical expertise on a single site by building new mineral water baths and, fortunately, plans for these were laid just prior to the First World War.

The plaster bust of the seventh Duke of Devonshire donated by its sculptor Mr W Gascombe-Johns in 1901. It was used to cast the bronze statue erected in Eastbourne.

Chiswick House on Marlborough Road was acquired by the hospital in 1913 and was used for a variety of purposes including research beds for the Manchester University Centre for the study of chronic rheumatism, flats for married staff and a nursing school for state enrolled nurses.

The two buildings considered by the Buxton Bath Charity in its search for hospital accommodation can be seen here. The Great Stables forming the Devonshire Hospital was the ultimate choice and is prominent on the left of this picture. To the right of the hospital is the Palace Hotel behind which is the Wye House Private Asylum on Corbar Hill, a design by Henry Currey of 1856 originally intended as patient accommodation to be built on Sylvan Park. In 1912 it became the Cavendish High School for Girls and in the early 1990s it was demolished and the site used for private housing.

DEVONSHIRE HOSPITAL

AND

BUXTON
BATH CHARITY:

INSTITUTED FOR THE

RELIEF OF POOR PERSONS

FROM ALL PARTS OF GREAT BRITAIN AND IRELAND,

SUFFERING FROM

RHEUMATISM, GOUT, SCIATICA, AND NEURALGIA; PAINS, WEAKNESS, OR
CONTRACTIONS OF JOINTS OR LIMBS, ARISING FROM THESE DISEASES, OR
FROM SPRAINS, FRACTURES, OR OTHER LOCAL INJURIES; CHRONIC FORMS
OF PARALYSIS; DROPPED HANDS, AND OTHER POISONOUS EFFECTS OF
LEAD, MERCURY, OR OTHER MINERALS; SPINAL AFFECTIONS; DYSPEPTIC
COMPLAINTS; AND UTERINE DISORDERS WHICH MAY DEPEND UPON A
RHEUMATIC OR GOUTY DIATHESIS.

SUPPORTED BY ANNUAL SUBSCRIPTIONS AND VOLUNTARY CONTRIBUTIONS.

ANNUAL REPORT

FOR THE YEAR 1914.

MEDICAL REPORT AND STATISTICS;
MANAGEMENT, HISTORY, ANNUAL STATEMENT, ACCOUNTS;
PRIVILEGES OF SUBSCRIBERS;
BYE-LAWS AND REGULATIONS FOR PATIENTS;
LIST OF SUBSCRIPTIONS, BENEFACTIONS, &c.;
AND METEOROLOGICAL REPORT FOR THE YEAR 1912.

BUXTON:
DERBYSHIRE PRINTING COMPANY, LTD., "HIGH PEAK NEWS" AND "ADVERTISER
OFFICES, MARKET PLACE.
1915.

CHAPTER FOUR
From Hospital to Centre of Excellence

New Hospital Baths

The new mineral water baths, built on the lower land adjoining the south front of the hospital, were completed during 1914 and in regular use by the end of the year. The baths were designed by the local architectural practice of Bryden and Walton.[115] This meant that the patients of the Bath Charity no longer had to make the journey from the hospital to the charity baths on George street and at the rear of the Old Hall Hotel, which, for the more severely infirm, would have been an arduous task. The new baths were fed with the natural mineral water from the 1882 drinking well on George street, by way of a large and very powerful gravity pump which was probably installed as part of the 1914 hospital baths project. The erstwhile Dr Robertson (1810-1897), former chairman of the hospital trustees, would have taken great exception to this move because of his belief that the efficacy of the water was adversely affected if it was used too far from the spring source. Opinions had changed since Robertson's death and it was now thought that such a move would have no bearing on the water's effectiveness. Due to the increased amount of steam required to heat the new baths and the poor state of the existing boiler the scheme also included the building of a new boiler house, new boilers and an upgrade of the hospital's heating system. The total cost of the project was £8551.

The patients now had in-house baths at the hospital which could be reached by a sloping walkway from the dome floor into a corridor which led through to a porch and door on the south front. The baths on either side of the corridor were symmetrical, mens to the west side, womens to the east, each set of baths containing plombiere, immersion, massage, douching and vapour baths, together with dressing boxes and a waiting area.[116] The building has been described thus:

> '...[It] occupies an eye-catching position on the downhill slope in front of the main building, and was designed with some attention to effect. A single-storeyed building with stone walls, it has a flat roof with an iron balustrade along the top of its front and side walls. The eleven-bay long front elevation has a projecting central porch with rusticated stonework and round-headed arches on its three outer sides and a segmental pediment to the front. Small, oval windows with keyed-in surrounds flank the porch, and the windows to either side have moulded and eared surrounds and sills on blocks. The windows at each end have double keyblocks, in contrast to the plain blocks of the other windows, and are set under triangular pediments on piers surmounted by urns* [117]

It is possible that at this time the opportunity was taken to extend the south-east doorway and its pedimented centrepiece by one bay. The detail of the original structure was faithfully maintained, indeed it is likely the original material was reused. The doorway was reset within a wide central ground-floor arched recess and retains the original inscription above:

> '...Let this tablet record the last munificent charity of William Spencer, 6th Duke of Devonshire, K.G. who allowed these buildings to be converted to the use of the sick poor, January A.D. 1858...'

The urn on the apex of the gable was formerly on St Ann's Drinking Well, designed by John Carr, in the Crescent. It was re-sited on the Devonshire Hospital after the well was demolished during the refurbishment of the Buxton Baths 1851-54. [118]

A 'whirlpool bath', having a rotating paddle in its base (an early version of the jacuzzi) was installed in the baths extension in 1917 at a cost of £95. This remained in situ, although largely unused in latter years, right up to the closure of the hospital in 2000. The origins of the large hydrotherapy pool which exists in the building today, date to 1952, when a pool was sunk as a response to the gradual transition from passive bathing to 'exercises in water' in the 1950s.[119] This pool was extended to its present size in 1957 and the smaller pool was sunk in 1979/80. Natural mineral water for drinking was also pumped to the hospital from the old drinking well on George Street and was dispensed to the patients from a counter, installed in about 1914, under the dome. Interestingly this water was pumped through narrow tubes inside the wider pipes carrying the water to the pools thus keeping the drinking water close to its temperature at the emergence from the spring.

Whirlpool bath.

Gravity pump in the old Devonshire Hospital drinking well on George street. This was installed c.1914 and was used to pump water up to the hospital after the opening of the new hospital baths. The pump remained in use, pumping water to the hospital hydrotherapy pools right up to its closure in 2000.

Soldiers at the Hospital

Unsettled times in Europe, culminating in the onset of World War One in 1914, concentrated minds at the hospital and resulted in the board of hospital trustees offering the War Office the use of 150 beds for sick and wounded soldiers. Their offer was accepted and by the end of the year the hospital had treated about 279 soldiers, suffering mostly from rheumatism and allied diseases.[120] Appeals from the board of management to subscribers to limit the use of their recommends during the period of the First War succeeded in liberating beds which could be used to treat discharged soldiers. During the period of the War, 5315 soldiers were treated and, although the hospital was initially closed for military patients in June 1919, the committee continued to reserve 100 beds at the request of the Ministry of Pensions for the treatment of their cases.[121]

Buxton had grown used to the presence of soldiers both during and immediately after the First World War when the town housed many discharged Canadian soldiers in the Granville Hospital at the Buxton Hydropathic Hotel on Hartington Road. [122] The last 86 soldiers to be treated at the hospital were discharged in 1919, to the Wharncliffe Military Hospital, Sheffield. To commemorate their last day in residence in Buxton a party of the soldiers visited the Opera House to see a matinee performance given by the Cricket Club. They were treated to a lavish tea under the great dome upon their return and were waited on by local volunteers.

A period of treatment at the Devonshire Auxiliary Military Hospital (AMH) did not necessarily mean being cooped up for lengthy periods inside a hospital ward. Patients were encouraged to keep as active as possible and those who were fit enough to get about had the freedom of the town and its facilities. A popular place to visit for the soldiers was the Hippodrome on St John's Road (formerly the Entertainment Stage, built 1889). At this time the building was being used as a cinema and a little poem written by Private F C Welsh during his stay describes his hospital routine including a visit to the 'Hipp'.

A DAY IN A.M.H.

The scene, it is Derbyshire, and Buxton is the place
where convalescent soldiers meet, their health and strength to brace

As I am amongst the flock, I'd like to draw your mind,
Just for a moment, to tell you how we are made at home, and treat so kind.

Auxiliary M.H. is our home and what a grand place too,
You find the sisters, nurses brisk with duties not a few.

At eight o'clock each morning, you hear the old bell ring,
To warn you "breakfast ready", which is fit for any king.

You then retire back to your ward, your toilet to complete
And receive your special treatment by the sisters, nice and neat.

We next return, again at noon, our appetites to ease,
With beef potatoes, rice and bread, and just eat what you please.

The afternoon is nicely spent, in visiting the Hipp,
And other various picture shows, which we are granted "Free Permit".

By the time the show is over, and the time we get back home,
A splendid tea is set for us when we hear, the old bell toll

At eight each night, there's service and the different vicars here
Gives us our numbers what to sing, then renders, a nice prayer.

Soon after that, the Matron with her basket on her arm
Each man provides with bacca, she sees no one miss their tum.

We hear again the old bell toll to tell us, it is time,
To go and get our supper, and be in bed by nine.

So now I think, I've done my best to tell you all I've known.
How each man's made so comfy, in our happy little home. [123]

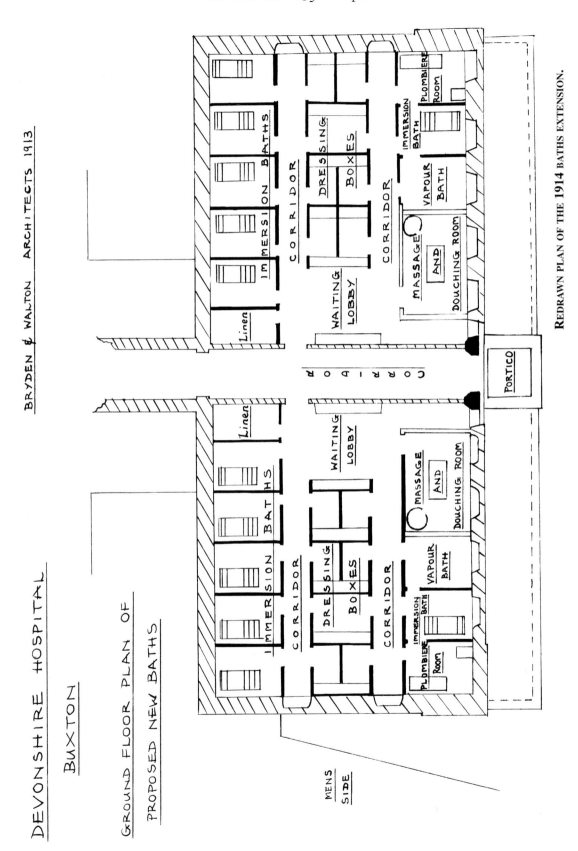

DEVONSHIRE HOSPITAL

BUXTON

GROUND FLOOR PLAN OF

PROPOSED NEW BATHS

BRYDEN & WALTON ARCHITECTS 1913

REDRAWN PLAN OF THE 1914 BATHS EXTENSION.

MENS SIDE

PORTICO

CORRIDOR

IMMERSION BATHS

Linen

CORRIDOR

DRESSING BOXES

WAITING LOBBY

CORRIDOR

MASSAGE AND DOUCHING ROOM

VAPOUR BATH

IMMERSION BATH

PLOMBIERE ROOM

Patients taking Buxton Water under the Dome.

1 Northleigh Villas in use as a Nurses' Home.

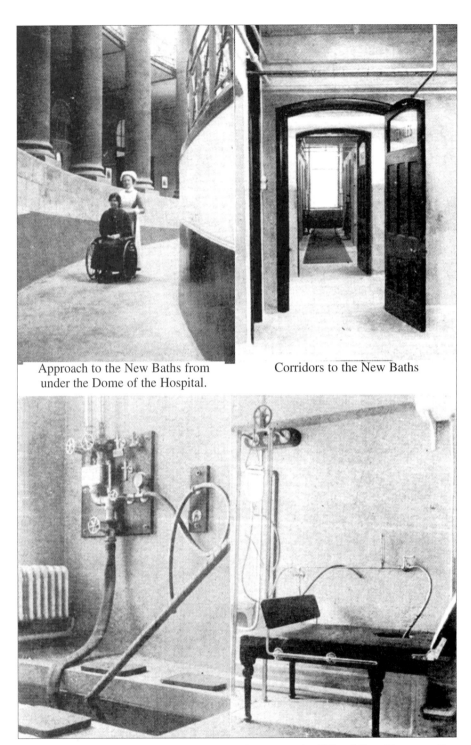

Approach to the New Baths from
under the Dome of the Hospital.

Corridors to the New Baths

One of the Buxton Mineral Water
Immersion Baths showing mixing
valves and douching apparatus.

Apparatus for "Plombières Treatment"
now in use at the Hospital.

A page of photographs in the Annual Report of 1914.

Patients with rheumatological and arthritic conditions were encouraged to keep moving around during their stay at the hospital so that their joints did not stiffen - a problem very familiar to sufferers of these conditions. The above poem makes it clear that this regime was pursued and, in fact, most of the ambulant patients spent their days out of the ward, carrying their treatment cards around with them. Their meals were taken in the patients dining room on the ground floor. For many of these patients, the only time they actually spent on the wards was at night.

Vera Brittain, pacifist, lecturer and writer, gives a description of life at the hospital during the four years beginning in 1915 during which she worked at the hospital as a V.A.D. nurse.

'...The hospital had originally been used as a riding school, but a certain Duke of Devonshire, with exemplary concern for the welfare of the sick but none whatsoever for the feet of its nursing staff, had caused it to be converted to its present charitable purpose. The main part of the building consisted of a huge dome, with two stone corridors running one above the other round its quarter-mile circumference. The nurses were not allowed to cross its diameter, which contained an inner circle reserved for convalescent patients, so that everything forgotten or newly required meant a run around the circumference. As kitchens, sink rooms and wards all lead off the circular corridors and appeared to have been built as far away from each other as possible, the continuous walking along the unresistant stone floors must have amounted, apart from the work itself, to several miles a day.

My hours there ran from 7.45am until 1pm, and again from 5.00pm until 9.15pm - a longer day, as I afterwards discovered, than that normally required in many army hospitals..... Meals, for all of which I was expected to go home, were not included in these hours. As our house was nearly half a mile from the hospital on the slope of a steep hill, I never completely overcame the aching of my back and the soreness of my feet throughout the the time that I worked, and felt perpetually as if I had just returned from a series of long route marches..' [124]

The new south front baths, 1914.

Treatment of Arthritis using Buxton Water and Vaccines

During the early part of the 20th Century the use of Buxton's natural mineral water was still believed to be of great benefit in the treatment of arthritis and rheumatic conditions. The Devonshire administered many of these treatments in the form of shallow baths and a range of douches. Although today there is considerably more scepticism about the water's properties, the basic premise used in these treatments was sound. It was thought that arthritic conditions could be relieved by improving the patient's general health. and this could be achieved by stimulating the body's own natural defences against disease and infection. This stimulation was achieved by the external application of, or ingestion of, the local water. In the 1920s medical researchers at the hospital carried out experiments on the patients to show the effectiveness of the Buxton water in gout, arthritis and rheumatic conditions. They published their findings in a small book in 1924. At Buxton great emphasis was still placed on the unique properties of the water itself, its constituent elements of calcium, nitrogen, argon and helium, and its striking blue colour and lack of unpleasant taste or smell. Buxton at this time advertised itself as 'the Spa of Blue Waters'.[125]

In 1933 Dr C.W. Buckley, an Honorary Physician, observed that Buxton was the larger of the three main 'Spa Hospitals' treating arthritic complaints, in that the Devonshire Hospital provided 300 beds compared with 158 at the Bath Royal Mineral Water Hospital, and 150 beds at Harrogate's Royal Bath Hospital and associated Rawson Convalescent Home.[126]

Dr Buckley also described the laboratory for chemical research, headed by a full-time bio-chemist, as a 'special feature' of the Devonshire Hospital services and, in cases where the medical condition did not respond to water treatment, recourse was made to the use of vaccines in order to *'...Wake up the tissues to make them destroy the offending organisms...'*[127]

The use of vaccines in the treatment of arthritis during the first half of the 20th century implies that medical science at that point believed the root cause of arthritis to be infective. Although it has not been disproved conclusively, this is not currently favoured. The use of the term 'vaccine' is interesting - it means the use of a dead or weakened version of an invading organism in order for the body to build up its own defences against the disease organism. This predisposes that the invading organism can be identified and isolated. There is no evidence of this and we must assume that they were using the term 'vaccine' in a loose sense only. Antibiotic drugs did not become widely available until the 1940s, after the discovery of penicillin by Alexander Fleming in 1928. Modern day drugs, some injected directly into the joints, go some way to relieving the condition now.[128]

Finance and Donations

Donations of a many and varied character were constantly being made to the charity, for example, walking sticks, pork pies, bandages, billiard tables, mixed nuts, coal and socks. The charity itself did not have enough regular income to supply these essentials to its patients and frequent donations of this kind were essential to the continuity of the hospital. The donation of an Aeolian pipe organ in 1931, by Mr Robert Whitehead JP, who was then chairman of the committee of management, stands out as one of the most generous. Mr Whitehead had donated a snooker table to the hospital in 1914 which became one of a pair of tables sited under the dome.[129] A particularly interesting gift, made in 1914 by the Duke of Devonshire, was the old drinking trough which had originally stood in the middle of the Great Stables before its conversion to the hospital. More interesting still is the recent excavation in about 1989 of a raised circular area in the tarmac surface of the hospital car park which

The Devonshire Hospital from Manchester Road in 1907.

The Buxton Douche Bath and 4 Needle Shower.

was found to be the buried base of the same trough!

The Devonshire Hospital and Buxton Bath Charity continued to be totally financed by subscriptions from the public. The list of regular subscribers remained lengthy, and being a subscriber remained an important act of philanthropy amongst the better-off people. The years of the First World War, however, saw some decrease in the amount subscribed to the charity, and regular appeals for money were made, pointing out that the average cost of each patient for a three week stay at the hospital amounted to around five times

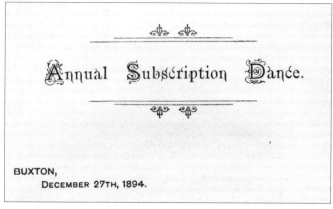

Invitation to the Annual Subscription Dance, 1894. All subscribers to the charity were entitled to bring along any number of friends to the dance providing they were not Buxton residents.

as much as the minimum subscription. All subscribers of under 4 or 5 guineas who admitted a patient were asked to provide a donation to make up this deficiency.[130]

Such was the demand for places at the hospital that the management board were always looking out for new ways of raising funds for the charity. Significant income was raised from an annual flag day and a subscription dance. The advent of the wireless opened a new opportunity to appeal for funds to a national audience and the Mayor of Buxton's appeal resulted in a notable increase in the numbers of subscribers to the charity and a large influx of extra donations.[131]

Patients gathered under the great dome in front of the plaster statue of the 7th Duke of Devonshire.

Entertainment for the Patients

By 1931 it was felt that the hospital should have its own cinema facilities and an appeal was initiated to raise £500 to buy the necessary projection equipment. The Co-operative Society provided the greater part of the money required and the target was soon met. By the following year work had been completed at a cost of £556 to install a projection box in the passage adjoining the patients dining room so that sound films could be shown. In 1959 the hospital purchased 35 mm projection equipment and cinemascope films were shown twice weekly. Television sets were installed in the rest rooms in the same year. There was a stage in the patients dining room which was used from the 1950s onwards for the annual pantomime. Staff revues were performed on the stage from the early 1970s. These performances were open to both patients and the public.

Two full sized snooker tables were sited in rooms off the dome and were later moved out under the dome and were available for use by both patients and staff. Radio DRH was founded in

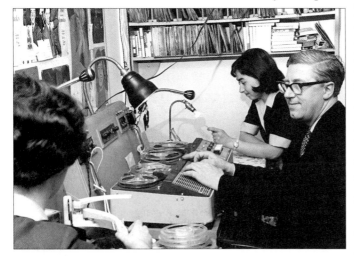

Radio DRH in operation, with the station's founder, Jim Dingle.

November 1963 and was run by voluntary staff. In its early days Radio DRH liaised with Leeds General Hospital who had their own in-house radio and were able to offer help and advice to the new station. Many of the presenters worked at the hospital during the day and did a stint on the radio during the evening. In addition to the usual music programmes there were regular record request shows, quizzes and interviews. The first hospital television station in the nation, DRH television, came into being in December 1972, with a broadcast of the annual staff revue from the patients dining room. Headsets for each patient were also installed in the wards during 1972 so that individuals could tune into the channels without disturbing others on the ward. Studios for both the radio and TV stations were housed in the basement of Clarendon House and live television shows were often filmed in the gymnasium. The station's broadcasts were relayed to the wards, first in black and white and after 1979 in colour. Outside television cameras covered the town's annual well dressing procession in July and presented it live to the wards as it passed the hospital.

The annual Well Dressings procession being filmed by DRH television in an outside broadcast.

Additions and Improvements

Surplus funds remaining in the hands of the British Red Cross after the end of World War One led to a grant of £8,000 to the Buxton Bath Charity. Work began in August 1920 in extending the hospital by building a large new dining room, equipping the kitchens, erecting and equipping a massage room, improving the laundry and renovating the plunge bath. Peter Pierce of Buxton was appointed as architect for the £23,799 scheme and the contract was placed in the hands of a local builder, Herbert Robinson of South Avenue. The remaining £15,799 was to be raised by public appeal. The commemoration stone for the new wing was laid on 29 October 1921 by H.R.H. Princess Mary. Raising the money for the building work balance by public subscription proved difficult; on completion of the project in 1923 £10,000 still remained to be found, and it was not until 1925, following further public appeals, that the remaining money was raised. The new extension housed the patient's dining hall on the ground floor with the upper floor providing kitchens and, initially the nurses' dining room. Later this was used by other staff, though as late as 1965 others dined in the basement of Clarendon House. [132]

The 1921 hospital extension from Manchester Road soon after its completion.

1926 saw the expenditure of £405 on new lavatory facilities, alterations to the Bacterial Department, dispensary and offices. In 1927 White's patent flooring was laid on the ground floor corridor surrounding the dome at a cost of £194. The same year saw the expenditure of £663 on new flooring underneath the large central area of the dome and this is probably the same maple flooring which existed at the closure of the hospital in 2000. Repairs were also made at this time to the flat parts of the roofing and the four cupolas surrounding the dome base at a cost of £2,776. [133]

Sometime during the 1920s the ceilings of some of the wards were under-drawn with false ceilings, covering up the old oak beams which had until then been exposed.[134] Some of the ward ceilings remained uncovered until after World War Two but all had been replaced with false ceilings by the early 1970s. This must have dramatically lowered the natural light levels in the wards as it cut off the light from the windows in the four cupolas. Before these changes the wards would have had been brightly lit by both ceiling and wall windows. Redecoration and repair of the dome was undertaken in 1929 at the cost of £493 and the dome interior has been decorated on several occasions since, a relatively costly operation due to its inaccessibility.

A new hospital laundry was built and equipped between 1929-31 at a cost of £3338. The existing laundry in George Street, adjoining the old Charity Hot Baths, had been in use for many years and was no longer considered to be hygienic. The architect for the alterations was Peter Pierce. This laundry continued to service the requirements of not only the Devonshire but all the hospitals in Buxton until its closure in January 1977 when all linen services were centralised at Stepping Hill Hospital, Stockport. The laundry buildings were converted into staff sitting rooms, cloakrooms, showers and toilets.

Royal recognition of the work carried out at the hospital was received in 1934 when King George V gave permission to use the word 'Royal' in the title of the hospital. The Devonshire Royal Hospital (DRH) had by now become a specialist hospital for patients in the north of the country and in 1942 advertised itself as a 'National Hospital for Rheumatism and Allied Diseases'.[135] The growing reputation of the hospital brought an increased demand for its the services and there was pressure to increase the treatment facilities and ward accommodation. In 1938 designs were created, by Sir Hubert Worthington of Manchester, to extend the hospital baths by the addition of a two-storey pedimented block at each end of the south front of the building. The extensions were to provide more dressing cubicles, rest rooms, bathing accommodation and wards on the first floor. The project was costed at £35,000 but never actually got off the ground due to the outbreak of war before tenders could be invited.[136]

Acquisitions

In 1946 plans were drawn up to convert Chiswick House into ward space, providing 37 research beds for long-stay patients requiring investigation and active treatment. These patients were to be referred to the hospital from the Manchester University Centre for the study of chronic rheumatism. It is not known how much of this work took place but Chiswick House was later used as flats for married staff and as a nursing school for state enrolled nurses. In more recent times the basement of the building was used as a storage area for medical records.[137]

The Devonshire Hospital and Buxton Bath Charity acquired the adjoining Corbar Hill Hydropathic Hotel Ltd, on Manchester Road, in 1930. Also known as Clarendon House it was converted from the Clarendon private lodging house in the early 1890s. It is reputed that a Roman bath was discovered in the land at the rear of this property in about 1880, although there is no firm evidence to support this claim.[138] During 1931 the building was connected to the hospital by a covered footbridge and was officially opened on 4th December 1931 by Robert Whitehead, JP, Chairman of the committee of management. This addition to the hospital was refurnished and decorated and used as accommodation for nursing and domestic staff. The total cost of this acquisition, including the conversion work, totalled £7,400. Further alterations totalling £272 were carried out in 1933. Clarendon House was used in the 1970s and 1980s as extra ward accommodation being known as Block 6. The visiting dental officer had his surgery in this block where he looked after the dentition of the inpatients at the hospital. Later still the Clarendon was used exclusively as administrative offices and lecture rooms.

The adjoining properties on the east side of the hospital, 1 and 2 Lismore Villas, were purchased in 1935, making the square of properties bordering Manchester, Marlborough and

Clarendon House. Acquired by the hospital in 1930, it was originally the Corbar Hill Hydropathic Hotel.

Devonshire roads the property of the hospital with the exception of the building on the corner of Marlborough Road and Devonshire Road (The Mount). The acquisition of Lismore Villas cost £1500 and the houses were converted into medical and nursing accommodation.

Annual reports show that the charity had been paying regular bills for furnishings, repairs and alterations at Corbar Hall on Manchester Road since 1940 and the building and grounds were purchased by the hospital in 1945 for £4077. Corbar Hall (originally Corbar Villa) was built by the architect Henry Currey in 1852 for a Blackburn brewer, Henry Shaw.[139] After refurbishment the hall was reopened as Buxton's maternity hospital, a function it continued to fulfil until its closure in 1986 when the maternity unit was re-sited in a purpose-built extension at Buxton Hospital, London Road.

Nursing accommodation was provided in 1959, when the Pendennis, a private hotel on Devonshire Road, was acquired by the NHS. Conversion through 1960 provided sleeping accommodation for 33, including eight bed-sitting rooms, and seven separate lounges, one each for visitors, staff nurses, matron, sisters, deputy matron, midwives, and domestics. The building was still occupied by the hospital in 1981 but later became the private Devonshire Nursing Home.[140]

The Buxton Clinic and Plans for Amalgamation

During the 1920s paying customers continued to take their bath treatments at the Hot and Natural Baths and the charity patients at the hospital baths. By the 1930s a group of businessmen identified a niche in the market for the middle class bather with limited means. In 1935 they opened the Buxton Clinic in the east wing of the Crescent, using the adjacent Hot Baths. Patients took a three week cure at the clinic, at a cost of four to six guineas weekly, which included the use of the baths, lounges, writing rooms, billiards and a library. The clinic was extended by the use of two further floors in 1938. In the 1950s the clinic still offered inclusive period tickets and received regular visits from football teams such as Manchester United, Nottingham Forest and Southampton, who took the Buxton Water treatment in order to prepare themselves physically for forthcoming matches.[141]

1945 marked the end of World War Two and the hospital board felt confident that it had handled well the extra pressure in six years of treating military patients. The management of the hospital were of the opinion that the Devonshire had more facilities for the treatment of rheumatic diseases than any other hospital in the country but the existing ward accommodation was in need of renovation and more room was required for medical staff and treatments. They accordingly put forward a proposal in December 1945 to demolish all the buildings adjoining the north of the hospital (Clarendon house, Chiswick House, Lismore Villas, Northleigh and Wyndholme) and to erect modern wards to house at least 400 patients, bringing the total patient accommodation to up to 700.

By this time the government's plans for the new health service were well advanced and it was perhaps because of this that representatives of the water treatment establishments took the opportunity to announce plans for a significant expansion of services. The plan was submitted in 1947 by the Buxton Co-ordinating Committee, a body consisting of the three main organisations in the town dealing with rheumatic complaints, namely, the Devonshire Royal Hospital, The Natural and Thermal Baths and the Buxton Clinic.[142] Their proposal was to set up a 'Rheumatism Centre' within the framework of the 1946 National Health Service Act, using the three institutions to provide a comprehensive range of treatments for sufferers of rheumatic conditions. The proposal also was to incorporate the 1945 extension plans for the Devonshire Royal Hospital (DRH) and increase the number of beds at the Buxton Clinic from 75 to 150, bringing the total number of beds up to over 800. The impetus for these proposals may have been rooted in discussion of possible collaboration, as early as 1937, between the three establishments and the Empire Rheumatism Council.[143]

The rheumatism centre would use the existing staff at the three institutions and suggested the addition of the following specialist staff and services: gynaecologist, neurologist, psychiatrist, anaesthetist, social worker, deep x-ray therapy unit, fracture clinic, vocational training centre (rehabilitation unit), a school of physiotherapy to train student members of the Chartered Society of Physiotherapy, an operating theatre block, so that patients need not be transferred to another hospital for the treatment of orthopaedic conditions and to expand the scope of the centre to include orthopaedic and postoperative conditions, a lecture theatre and classrooms at the hospital for student, postgraduates and physiotherapists.

This was by any reckoning, an ambitious plan and its proponents were very aware of the cost implications of the project and the many difficulties they would encounter during its development. In the event the Rheumatism Centre never got off the drawing board, perhaps due to a combination of lack of funds and a lack of will on the part of the government who were on the point of absorbing the hospital into the National Health Service.

Hydrotherapy in the 1950s.

Excavation of the base of the horse drinking trough from the hospital car park in about 1989. A circular impression under the tarmac surface of the car park had intrigued the hospital engineer for many years, resulting in this discovery. The base can still be seen displayed in the south car park. The trough had been in regular use before the building was converted into hospital.

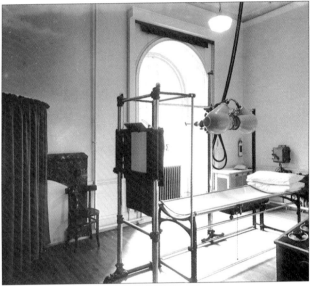

Buxton Clinic X-ray theatre.

Buxton Clinic Physiotherapy room in the east wing of the Crescent.

A corner of the research laboratories as they appeared in 1932.

Plans by the Buxton Co-ordinating Committee in 1947, for a proposed new 'Rheumatism Centre'

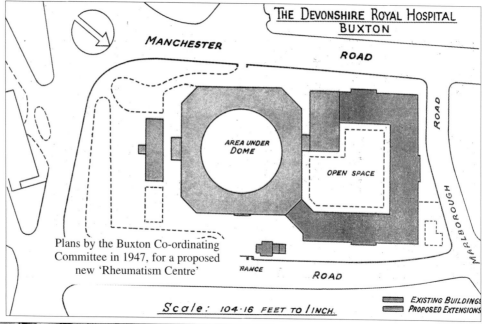

THE DEVONSHIRE ROYAL HOSPITAL
BUXTON

MANCHESTER ROAD

AREA UNDER DOME

OPEN SPACE

RANCE ROAD

MARLBOROUGH ROAD

Scale: 104·16 FEET TO 1 INCH.

EXISTING BUILDINGS
PROPOSED EXTENSIONS

Plans by the Buxton Co-ordinating Committee in 1947, for a proposed new 'Rheumatism Centre'

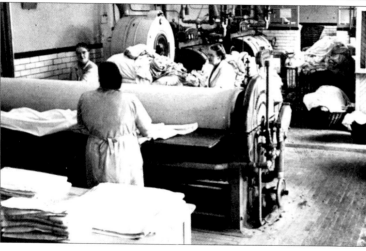

The Laundry in the 1950s.

The Coming of the National Health Service

By 1945 the government's plans for the establishment of the National Health Service were being drawn up. The Devonshire, like all other independent hospitals, was to be absorbed into the new system and come under state control. All in all the government became responsible for 1143 voluntary hospitals with over 90,000 beds, and 1545 municipal hospitals with 390,000 beds. The committee of management were aware of the coming changes and plans were made to provide a specialist medical service in the new system, using the fields in which it had built its reputation. A close liaison was established with the University of Manchester which was thought to be of great value to both parties, particularly from the research point of view.

So it was that the Devonshire Royal Hospital and Buxton Bath Charity ceased to be a charity on 1st April 1948 when it came under the control of the Ministry of Health body serving the north western area of the country. After 1948 the Buxton Clinic became annexed as part of the Devonshire Royal Hospital and the clinic finally closed its doors in June 1963, in line with the slump in the use of water treatments nationally. [144]

For about the first ten years as a National Health Service hospital, the Devonshire was managed by the South Manchester hospital authorities, but for most of its time it was run by the Stockport Area Health Authority, under the Stockport and Buxton Hospital Management Committee, and more latterly by the Stockport Acute Services NHS Trust. The other two hospitals in the town, the Buxton and Cavendish Hospitals, although originally managed by the same authority, were run by administrators from Chesterfield and North Derbyshire from 1974.[145] The reason the Devonshire did not change over to management from North Derbyshire is probably due to its historical roots in that the vast majority of patients treated at the unit were from the North West of the country and most of the consultants also worked in Manchester and Stockport, but also Stoke on Trent. There was also a continuing link with Manchester University.

Medical & Surgical Specialities

As with all hospitals, the Devonshire was a conglomeration of many separate departments serving the patient in different ways. But through the 20th century, significant medical advances saw different specialisms emerging and progressively more influence being placed on interdisciplinary work in the treatment of patients.

Nursing

A mixture of orthopaedic, rheumatology and medical wards housed the patients at the hospital and a large number of nurses and auxiliary staff were required to give the 24 hour care needed. It is often said that nursing is a vocation and this is well exemplified in the Devonshire Hospital history. Nursing has never been a well remunerated job and yet great demands are made on its practitioners. During the early days of the Devonshire many of the nurses and auxiliaries performed the job as unpaid volunteers and this was so during the period of the First World War. A strict hierarchical system kept the nursing staff 'in their places', a situation dramatically expressed by Vera Brittain during her nursing spell at the hospital as she describes the sister-in-charge of her ward:

> *'...A weather beaten, dry little woman, with hard brown eyes and a fussy manner, she had a habit of tight-lacing which made her appear aggressively out of proportion. Her aitches, though right numerically, were wrongly distributed, and I had difficulty in maintaining the correct expression*

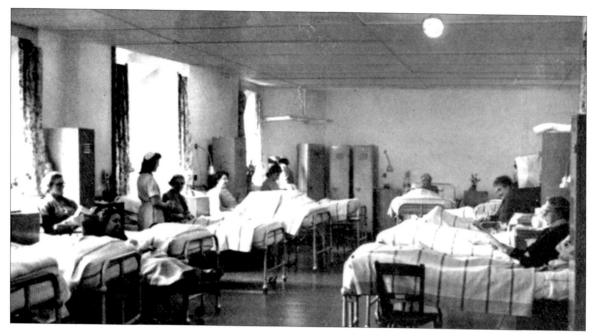

Hospital beds in the 1950s

Architect's impression of the proposed new hospital south front, 1937/8, designer Sir Hubert Worthington of Manchester.

of disciplined composure when she forcibly inquired , as she did every evening; "Narse! have you given 'Ibbert his haspirin?" When she wanted to address me she always shouted "Narse!" except when she tried to use my name. This she invariably got wrong, although it seemed to me to be simple enough to remember-particularly in wartime, when we were all so patriotic. Her distrust of V.A.D. probationers was evident from the first, but this was counterbalanced by a determination even greater than my own to make me maid-of-all-work.

"I've been a narse for seventeen yahs and a Sistah for twelve," she informed me ominously when I protested at being told for the second time to dust a ward which, as part of the ordinary morning's routine, had been finished hours before...'[146]

The great majority of the inpatients were suffering significant pain from their rheumatic and arthritic conditions and, for a number, restricted mobility and increased body weight due to lack of exercise. This degree of disability makes nursing such patients heavy and demanding work, but much kindness was always demonstrated and great care was taken by the nursing staff to preserve the patient's dignity when undergoing intimate procedures. During the 1970s and 1980s the Devonshire wards were grouped into 'blocks' depending on the type of patients treated. Blocks One and Three housed rehabilitation patients, Block Two orthopaedics, Blocks Four and Five rheumatology. After this time the 'block' grouping was dropped and the wards were categorised according to the type of case e.g. Orthopaedic wards, etc. A 12 bedded head injury ward was opened in Spring 1981 to care for patients suffering from brain damage. The patients had received their more critical care at larger acute hospitals and were transferred to the Devonshire once their condition had stabilised.

Surgery

An operating room was included in the accident provision of 1897 and, despite the opening of the Buxton & District Cottage Hospital in 1912, surgical cases were handled through the First World War and beyond. Such cases were related to diseases of the locomotor system with which the hospital had strong expertise, for example, the Annual Report for 1932-33 records fractures and dislocations and reference to a knee operation. It is possible that surgical intervention diminished to some degree during the middle of the 20th century, until techniques of joint replacement began to be developed.[147] In 1959 a new orthopaedic theatre was constructed, where, in addition to the more routine

orthopaedic surgical procedures, the specialism of joint replacement surgery was performed from about 1970. The joint replacement programme conducted hip replacements, using the famous prosthesis developed by Professor John Charnley (1911-82) in about 1960 at Manchester Royal Infirmary. The Charnley prosthesis was a significant advance on its predecessors, using a much smaller ball-head to move in the nylon socket which was fitted in the acetabulum of the pelvis. The larger part of the joint was inserted into the top of the femur using bone cement (low

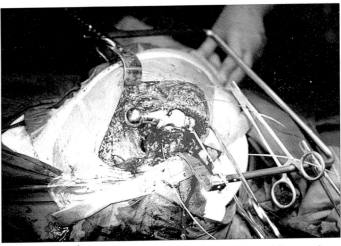

Hip replacement at the Devonshire. The head of the stainless steel prosthesis can be seen fitted into the shaft of the femur (thigh bone).

friction arthroplasty). The new joint, due to its smaller head size, resulted in less friction between the two opposing surfaces and therefore considerably extended the life of the replacement. Adaptations of the Charnley joint are still being fitted but advances in the design of the metalwork have dispensed with the need for bone cement which was always a potentially weak point. In addition to hips other joint replacements were developed and fitted at the Devonshire including knees, shoulders, finger and toe joints.[148] In 1972 the operating theatre closed for significant refurbishment during which time operations were performed in a operating theatre tent of the type used by mobile army surgical units. The tent was erected in the old gymnasium which was sited immediately to the right of the hospital's main entrance, between the outpatients department and the WRVS shop at the bottom of the right staircase. The gymnasium was temporarily moved during this process to the patients dining room where it was later to take up permanent residence.

Another significant interruption to the surgical programme was avoided in about 1986 when the theatre underwent a complete rebuild in order to conform with more modern conditions of sterility. The theatre was closed for about one year and surgery continued in another tent which was erected in the gymnasium (the patients' dining room until the 1970s). The temporary theatre was of the positive internal pressure type, which drew filtered air into the tent thus reducing the risk of infection from airborne microbes. Separate enclosures led off from the tent to serve as recovery and anaesthetic rooms. Despite the obvious inconvenience the tent served the surgeons well during this difficult period and the surgery workload was hardly altered, the joint replacement programme continuing as if nothing had happened. Unfortunately the parquet flooring of the gymnasium suffered from the effects of the antistatic matting laid on it and the floor was later relaid with vinyl.

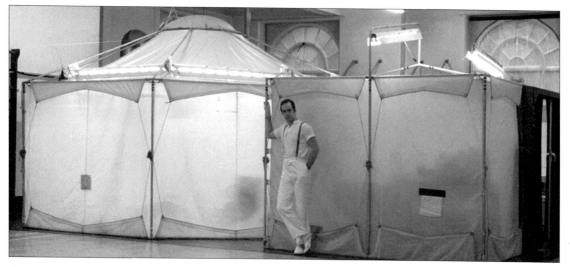

The temporary theatre tent which was erected in the patients gymnasium during the major theatre upgrade in about 1986. The main operating chamber is in the domed area on the left whilst the square portion on the right functioned as an anaesthetic/recovery room. Standing in front of the structure is theatre porter, Myles Burgess.

Surgery returned to the newly refurbished theatre in 1987 which had been uprated with all the modern features of enhanced sterility in order to keep infection rates as low as possible. The same project also included the removal of the theatrical stage from the patient's dining room. This area was first used as changing rooms and a rest room for the temporary operating theatre, and subsequently as additional patients' bathrooms.

Radiology

The first X-ray equipment was installed at the hospital in 1912 and was the responsibility of the clinical pathologist. The 1914 annual report states that it was proving very useful in achieving accurate diagnoses and that the equipment was also being used to actually treat some conditions. The report does not specify which conditions were considered to be responsive to topical irradiation, but, certainly, localised exposure of an arthritic joint to x-radiation would have had the effect of reducing inflammation. Today's knowledge of the potential hazards of low level radiation exposure make this practise seem somewhat irresponsible but we have the benefit of hindsight and irradiation of this nature was not at all uncommon at the time. Radiotherapy is still in use today, usually in the treatment of malignant tumours but the type of radiation used and the administration of the treatment are very carefully calculated and regulated.

The equipment was replaced in 1929 with a Victor Wantz junior X-ray set with a rotary disc rectifier. Photographs of the equipment in use show very little, if any protection from scattered radiation or electric shock from high tension cables.[149] This equipment remained in place until 1939 when a personal donation of £1000 from the chairman of the trustees, Lady Turner, enabled the purchase of a considerably advanced X-ray set which featured four valve rectification and much improved protection from radiation exposure and electrical shock. Alterations to the structure of the X-ray department were also made at this time at a cost of £173.[150] Later equipment, supplied by the Dean X-ray equipment manufacturers was installed which had fluoroscopic features, enabling the body to be viewed in 'real time' via the x-ray image on a phosphorescent screen in a darkened room. This equipment remained in place until the department underwent a complete overall and re-equipping with General Electric Co. (GEC) gear in 1981 which, in addition to normal radiographic functions, used fluoroscopy linked to closed circuit television to display images in barium contrast examinations. This equipment remained functional until the closure of the hospital in 2000. Throughout its existence the X-ray department was staffed by a single radiographer and a clerical assistant. Radiologists from Stepping Hill Hospital made regular visits to interpret the accrued X-ray images and issue reports to the referring doctors.

Out-Patient Clinics

The outpatient department held regular clinics in the fields of orthopaedics, rehabilitation, rheumatology, ophthalmology, psychiatry, clinical psychology and fitting of surgical appliances. These clinics received both inpatients and outpatients referred from the local general practitioners. Visiting consultants from Stepping Hill Hospital and Manchester joined with the resident nursing staff to provide these clinics. Working closely with the orthopaedic and rheumatology clinics was the small plaster theatre on the first floor of the hospital where specialised plasters were made and fitted according to instructions by the consultants. A small team of nurses and auxiliary staff ran this unit

Pathology & Pharmacy

Pathology services were provided from a laboratory at the hospital. The laboratories were updated in 1932-3 at a cost of £254. Requests for their services were received from the hospital's own doctors and the local general practitioners. The work carried out involved microbiology, haematology and blood transfusion. The more complex forms of haematology, clinical chemistry and histopathology were dealt with at Stepping Hill Hospital. A small dispensary was housed at the hospital staffed by

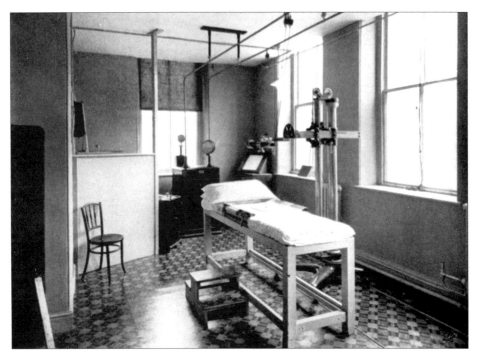

Victor Wantz Junior X-ray set. Installed in 1929 it was in improvement on its predecessor, having a rotating anode which was capable of handling the heat generated during the production of x-rays and a greater output and penetrating power. Compared with the today's standards, the protection from radiation and electric shock provided here, to patient and operator, is virtually non-existent.

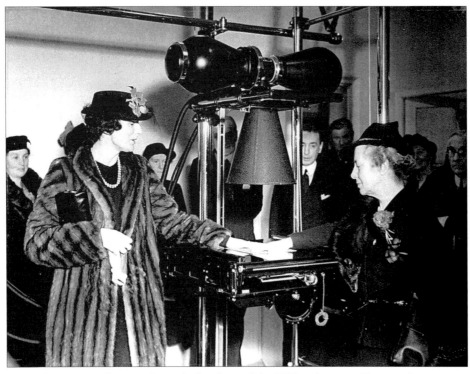

Lady Turner and companion at the handover of the 1939 replacement X-ray equipment.

in-house pharmacists. They supplied drugs to both in and out-patients, who had been seen at the hospital, and also to the other hospitals in the town.

Physiotherapy and Hydrotherapy

The profession of physiotherapy has it origins in the much earlier practitioners, known as medical rubbers, galvanists or anatomical shampooers. In Buxton the medical rubbers were either seasonal visitors or residents in the town. Mrs Ainsley of Sheffield practised in the season from 1826 and J. Whalley and Son from 1835. By 1855 Joseph Miller, Shampooer and Professor of the water cure, had set up a resident hydropathic house on Hall Bank which dispensed the cold water cure treatment. The early practitioners of medical rubbing contained some unscrupulous operators and in order to protect the reputation of the profession the Society of Trained Masseuses was founded by four nurses in 1894. In Buxton the term rubber was replaced by masseur in 1890.[151] The society held regular examinations and published rules of conduct in order to maintain high standards and by 1900 it acquired the legal status of a professional organisation and became the Incorporated Society of Trained Masseuses. The society was granted a royal charter in 1920 and it amalgamated with the Institute of Massage and Remedial Gymnastics to become the Chartered Society of Massage and Medical Gymnastics. The present name, the Chartered Society of Physiotherapy (CSP) was adopted in 1942.[152]

The Devonshire massage department was opened in 1902 and was staffed by one honorary masseur. By 1904 the department had three hon. masseurs, two hon. masseuses and a hon. consulting electrical engineer who dispensed the electro-water treatments.[153] The hospital developed its own school of massage which gave a full course of training in massage, medical gymnastics, electrical and light treatments. In 1932 the school had 17 students undergoing training.[154] The department developed over the years, growing in size, eventually becoming the department of physiotherapy in about 1942. The hospital trained its own physiotherapists from this time until 1949/50 when the physiotherapy school was moved to Withington Hospital, Manchester. The student physiotherapists were accommodated at Corbar Hall up to 1945 and at Clarendon House for the remaining years until the move to Withington. The physiotherapists had the use of a gymnasium for the exercise of the more mobile patients. Many of the inpatients at the hospital needed regular physiotherapy due to the nature of their conditions and hence a large number of staff were needed to provide their treatment. The department also provided an outpatient service for people in the surrounding area.

The electrical department was under the control of the physiotherapists and a large room was allocated for the dispensing of electrical treatments. These included the four cell Schnee bath, arthromotor, mechanical vibrators, galvanic, Faradic and sinusoidal currents, electrical massage, electrical cautery and radiant heat baths.[155] On a postcard to his cousin at Atherton, Manchester, a patient wrote, in 1934:

> '...I am doing all right just been and had a massage bath, I have treatment every day, electric one day and massage and needle bath the other and they put me through it but I am pleased to say I am feeling better. They have something going on every night, we have talkies on Wednesday and they are good, better than the Savoy...'

An ultraviolet light treatment department was opened in the physiotherapy unit in 1935 which was used to treat skin conditions in patients of all ages and as a general tonic to children. This mode of treatment soon declined in popularity but some patients found it valuable right up to closure.

Devonshire Hospital Massage School 1932.

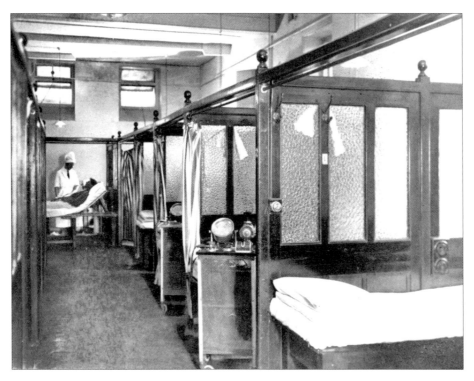

Devonshire Hospital Massage Department 1932.

As time passed the range of electrical treatments provided changed but these were a major element of physiotherapy until the 1970s.

In the 1960s and 1970s a regular sight under the dome was the daily 'group physiotherapy' sessions. This involved up to 30 patients at a time in a ring surrounding a central physiotherapist leading a gentle exercise session.[156] All patients, including the wheelchair-bound, were able to take part in these sessions which basically required them to copy the actions of the 'physio' as part of their general therapy. The physiotherapy component of these sessions may not have been very scientifically based but this was of little importance since most of the circle seemed to thoroughly enjoy it. For those who were confined to the wards a smaller, scaled down version of the process was carried out, again on a daily basis in most of the wards.

Group physiotherapy under the Dome.

The hospital was founded as part of the centuries old tradition of treating patients using the natural mineral water, and hydrotherapy was applied to a wide range of disorders. In the early part of the 20th century immersion baths, vapour baths, the Buxton massage bath, needle baths, the plombiere douche, the whirlpool bath and the steam douche were all used. At this time treatment was overseen by Bath Attendants (not physiotherapists). During this period the total number of treatments in the hydrotherapy, electrical, and massage departments rose from 37,738 in 1924 to 125,515 in 1945. From the 1940s onward, active rehabilitation grew in importance affecting both physiotherapy and hydrotherapy treatment. This brought physiotherapists into the baths to direct 'exercises in water' and led to the construction, in 1952, of a larger pool in place of some of the immersion baths. In 1957 this was extended to form the larger of the two pools which still exist within the hospital. The other was built in 1979-80 to provide additional facilities for the Head Injury Ward. Treatment in the water was always popular with the patients who found that they could achieve so much more in exercising with its support. John Lea, a paralysed polio patient at the hospital in the 1950s describes the treatment he received in the hydrotherapy unit:

'...Three mornings a week I went with the same physiotherapist down to the baths where a harness was slipped under me. I was swung from my bed high over the wall to be lowered gently into the water. It is hard to explain the feeling of fear that first time - regardless of the reassurance from very capable staff - of helplessness as I dangled in mid-air before being lowered into the pool. Although the physiotherapist was supporting me in only four foot six inches of water, when I floated free of that harness I desperately gripped the handrail. I found that miraculously, as my helpless feet sank to the bottom, I could stand on them. I did little more that first day than marvel at the experience but in later sessions Miss Sweatman developed my exercises.

The pool was filled with natural spring water that was piped under the town from the old baths in St George's Street [sic]. It is claimed to be more buoyant than ordinary water and to have many rejuvenating properties both as a drink and to bathe in. To allow the minerals to seep into our bodies we (staff included) never wiped ourselves dry but were always wrapped in warm towels and left to lie relaxed for thirty blissful minutes...' [157]

Mr Lea was admitted to the hospital in a completely paralysed state but was able to walk out after a period of some months - a tribute to the hard work of the hospital staff.

A hydrotherapy school was set up at the hospital to provide qualified physiotherapists with a six-month post-registration course covering exercises in water, alternating and contrast douching, spray massage and passive bathing. The school ran from May 1957 to May 1975 and just over 150 students passed through the school, over one third of them staying on at the Devonshire as part of the physiotherapy team. Up to 1966 the school prepared its students for examination and registration by the CSP but after this time exercises in water were included in the basic physiotherapy syllabus and the CSP ceased to register and examine hydrotherapists. After 1966 the students at Buxton were examined by resident consultant medical staff in conjunction with the Principal of the Bath School of Physiotherapy. The closure of the school brought an end to the separate management of hydrotherapy. It was amalgamated with the Physiotherapy department under the Superintendent Physiotherapist.

Occupational and Speech Therapy

An Occupational Therapy (OT) department was opened in 1943 when armed-forces staff were referred to the hospital for rehabilitation. The department was one of the pioneers in its field and from small beginnings it eventually housed a large rehabilitation kitchen with different worktop heights, a bathroom, two workshops and an 'aids for daily living' room. Other activities carried out in O.T. included woodworking, printing and even work on large weaving looms which were positioned under the dome.

Although not directly under the control of the occupational therapists, there were regular painting classes during the 1970s at the hospital. 'Arts for Health' was a more recent movement to encourage the patients and staff to try their hands at painting and sculpture. This group was responsible for various murals and a decorated wooden obelisk positioned in the middle of the dome

Occupational therapy was responsible for the development of handy domestic gadgets to help the disabled perform the routine day to day tasks which the physically fit take for granted. Devices ranged from grips to remove jar tops and devices to ease the holding of table irons by arthritic hands, to grabbing handles which help people who are unable to bend put on socks and stockings. In recent years such devices were on direct sale to the public from the hospital.

A large heated outdoor greenhouse, donated by the hospital's League of Friends, was also available for the patients, together with an assessment flat for the use of patients being considered for return to their own homes after a period of treatment. The Northwest Co-operative Society donated a minibus to the hospital in 1972 which was used to take patients out on home assessment visits, and bring members of the stroke club to their regular meetings at the hospital.

Speech therapy is a relatively recent introduction to the medical armoury and, although the speech therapy unit at the hospital was very small, it provided a valuable service. Patients with neurological problems, strokes and brain injuries are often left with communication problems. The speech therapist can assess the problem and advise on treatment. Swallowing and feeding impairment problems are also assessed and treated by the speech therapist.

Social Services

The welfare of patients housed at all of the three hospitals in Buxton was looked after by a social worker based at the Devonshire. After 1974 the hospital social worker liaised with social security, housing and social services during a patient's period of hospital care. Regular visits to the hospital were also made by chiropodists, dentists and opticians to meet patient needs.

Support Services

The main kitchen on the first floor of the hospital, opened in 1923, provided the catering services for both patients and staff. A large number of meals were prepared by a team of chefs and catering assistants. The kitchen underwent a major upgrading in 1982 when new kitchen fittings and apparatus were installed.

The works department, headed by the hospital engineer, attended to the regular maintenance. On hand were a team of joiners, bricklayers, decorators, electricians and plumbers. As with many old buildings, the hospital required regular maintenance and the building needed specialist attention in order to assess the integrity of complex structures such as the dome roof.

The portering department dealt with the transport of patients throughout the hospital, the distribution of post and supplies and the manning of the reception desk, amongst many other tasks The domestic services kept the hospital clean and tidy, including the residential staff accommodation.

Behind the scenes in every hospital there is an army of clerical and administrative workers preparing the paperwork necessary in patient care nowadays. These essential workers only become apparent to the public when things go wrong. The Devonshire clerical staff were positioned in various departments throughout the hospital, in offices and cellars and the lodge, preparing notes, x-rays and laboratory tests for the many clinics.

Voluntary organisations also played their part at the hospital. The in-house shop was run by the Women's Royal Voluntary Service, selling refreshments and much more to both patients and visitors. A small library service was provided weekly by the WRVS. The League of Friends of the Devonshire Royal Hospital was established in 1970 and raised funds which, over the years, were used to purchase key items of equipment. The Friends, who had the Duke of Devonshire as their patron, also organised the biennial 'Hyperfair', which was held in the hospital.

The spiritual needs of the hospital were met by visiting chaplains of different denominations and a small chapel was provided on the ground floor for regular weekly services and quiet prayer.

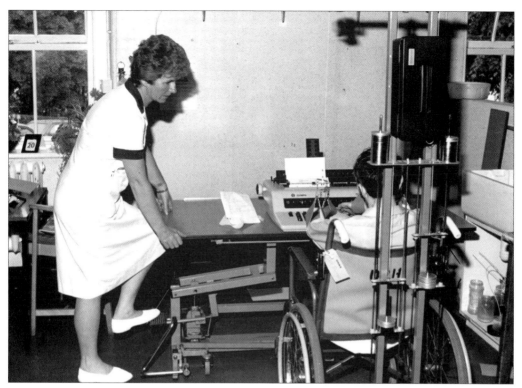

Occupational therapy. OT Susan Allan helping a wheelchair bound patient.

Opening of the large greenhouse for the use of patients and donated by the hospital's League of Friends.

ARRIVAL

ASSISTANCE

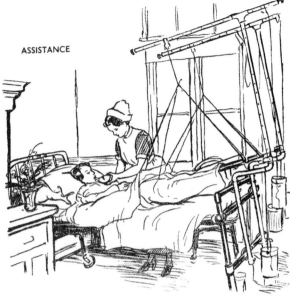

TAKING BUXTON'S
HEALING WATERS

DEPARTURE

Closure and the High Peak Health Forum

The idea of rationalising work at the Devonshire and a gradual move of its services to hospitals closer to the area of coverage, in and around Stockport, was first talked about in the 1980s and gradually gained in momentum. The DRH had always been something of an anomaly, being run from Stockport mainly for Stockport people. It was argued by the Stockport authority that it was more sensible to treat patients closer to their homes.

By the mid 1990s it was clear that the future of the Devonshire Royal Hospital (DRH) was in serious doubt. The introduction of a competitive ethos in the NHS meant that hospital managers were looking more and more carefully at costs. The main local use was by about 13,000 outpatients who visited the DRH annually. Above all, the greatest asset of the hospital, the central dome, was seen as providing an inefficient circular layout for a modern hospital and the use of notional leasing costs by the NHS, which was based on floor area, put the building at a serious disadvantage.

In the summer of 1995, DRH outpatient, Rene Wright of Chapel-en-le-Frith, along with husband Doug, organised a 'Save the Devonshire' petition. It reached 14,000 signatures before being handed to High Peak MP, Charles Hendry. In September of the same year, the GMB trades union called a public meeting at Buxton's Methodist Church to discuss the prospect of closure. There was a further meeting at the same venue a month later, called by the Community Health Council, the health watchdog organisation. No course of action could be discussed as no definite closure plans had been put forward. In December, a public consultation document was issued by Stockport Health Authority, the purchasers of health provision under the 'Thatcher' concept of a competitive NHS. The document, which was based upon an Estates Review prepared by Rawlinson, Kelly and Whittlestone, advocated closure. This followed on from the Finnamore Consulting Company's 'High Peak Estates Review', which had been commissioned as early as 1992. The public consultation document asked for a response by 31 March 1996. [158]

Two local men decided that the time was now right to mount a serious campaign to challenge Stockport Health Authority. Michael Bryant, DRH Superintendent Physiotherapist, had received permission from hospital management to explain the facts behind the closure issue to local people and organisations. Trevor Gilman had been a volunteer since 1982, initially with an organisation involved in rehabilitation called REMAP, later working with Mike Bryant in hospital television.[159] They had discussed a potential campaign as early as 1993, but could do nothing until a definite plan for closure had emerged. Trevor Gilman had formed 'The Buxton Group' in 1991 in response to the closure of the the Georgian Crescent and had taken over the chairmanship at the November 1995 AGM, so was in a position to muster that Group's resources.

It was realised immediately that to have any chance of success, the campaign must have the involvement and support of the local community. With the Buxton Group as a core it was decided to set up a meeting of all local organisations. An invitation list was compiled which included representatives of the three doctors' practices, the three chaplains, three borough councillors and the two county councillors, three trades unions, and many local organisations including the Civic Association, Leagues of Friends of the three Buxton hospitals, Rotary, Round Table, the Buxton Chamber of Trade, Tourist Association, Soroptomists, Business & Professional Womens' Club, and the local police. The meeting took place at the Old Hall Hotel on 31 January 1996. Nearly everyone invited attended, despite the atrocious weather - there was clearly widespread concern.

The meeting opened with a presentation of the choices faced by the health authorities, and an explanation of the way in which the closure proposal had emerged. A two hour discussion followed at the end of which it was clear that there were two separate major issues for the town; the effect on health provision, and the closure of another important town centre building. The first priority was clear - there should be a concerted response to the public consultation document. The representatives agreed to report back to their various organisations, and a second meeting was arranged for 15 February when the 'High Peak Health Forum' was formed. The stated aims of the Forum were:

1 To respond to the public consultation exercise on the future of hospital services in the area
2 To put views to the public alongside those of other interested parties
3 To examine closely the facts and financial figures behind North Derbyshire Health Autoritity's decision not to use the DRH building as a Community Hospital and to see if a solution could be found that matched more closely the best interests of local people.

The first move was to ask for more time to form a response to the public consultation document. This led to a delay in the deadline for response until 30 April. A public meeting was arranged on 24 April in which patients and public were able to question a panel of representatives of health management from Stockport and North Derbyshire. At the meeting, all of the members of the panel agreed that they would talk to the Forum Management Committee on a regular basis to discuss alternative proposals being identified by public consultation, and progress towards whatever changes that were imminent. The chief executive of Stockport Health Authority said that there would be no instant closure at the end of the consultation period, and indicated that the changes might be delayed while new information and ideas were considered. The Forum's response to the public consultation, entitled *A Single Community Hospital*, was submitted just before the 30 April deadline. Recognising Stockport Health Authority's desire to move services towards Stockport, but that thousands of patients from the Buxton area were treated annually at DRH, the central proposal was that all Buxton hospital services should be moved to the DRH site. At the end of April, High Peak Borough Council voiced their support to retain the DRH as a centre of excellence for the whole region.

The first meeting between the High Peak Health Forum and the health authorities took place at the Old Hall Hotel at the end of May 1996. This meeting set the pattern for a number of others over the next two years under the chairmanship of a local resident and magistrate, Dr John Cassidy. Health managers asked that the Forum arguments in favour of a single community hospital received the same scrutiny as their own, and offered help with background information on costings. At the beginning of this process, the services provided by all of the Buxton hospitals was included in discussions of alternative future provision. The closure of the DRH was delayed again and again as uncertainty meant that replacement facilities were not being made available anywhere. As well as meeting health chiefs, Forum members held regular meetings with other key figures including Charles Hendry MP for High Peak and, from the change in government in spring of 1997, Labour MP Tom Levitt, who had joined the forum previously when a County Councillor.

During this time the Forum developed as a bona fide representative organisation and had to set itself up with a constitution and audited finances. All of these matters, including production of regular newsletters, were handled by councillor and later Mayor of the Borough of High Peak, Jane McGrother. The Forum worked consistently to achieve its aims, holding regular meetings and seeking publicity through local radio and television and by the MPs raising questions in parliament and to ministers. Progressively other groups using the DRH joined in support of the Forum.

The persuasive task facing the Forum was always seen as one that transcended a single government department. The Health Minister was obviously involved, and received representations, either direct or through the MP, but the Heritage Minister was also involved, as this department would be expected to pay some costs for the building, whatever its use. The Transport Secretary's initiative to reduce car journeys also had a bearing on the issue, as removing services to a distance would result in more car usage.

One flaw in the Forum's argument was that the Lottery rules would not allow funding of the Health Service in any way. This was because of early fears that the National Lottery might be used as a source of government funds - as another tax in effect. English Heritage began to take a close interest in the future of the building in anticipation of its closure. A meeting of concerned parties was held at the DRH on 21 November 1996 after which it became clear that, because of its expected closure, the ownership of the building had been retained by the Secretary of State rather than being transferred to a Health Trust. As a means of overcoming the lottery problem, the Forum put forward the suggestion of dividing the maintenance of the site such that English Heritage would take responsibility for the fabric of the listed buildings. The possibilities of obtaining grants from the Lottery Heritage Fund for an alternative use was explained. NHS Estates were to liaise with English Heritage at every stage in the disposal process, and there had to be a smooth transition from the current owner to the next.

The end to the campaign was signalled in a report by NHS Estates and English Heritage, received by the Forum at the end of August 1997. It confirmed that North Derbyshire intended to provide the DRH services at various centres throughout the High Peak, and requested that Health Minister, Alan Milburn, support the recommendations. It also recommended that the efforts of NHS Estates and other bodies be directed to finding an alternative use for the site. At a board meeting on 16 September, North Derbyshire Health Authority confirmed their decision to take services from the DRH.

The Forum held its last meeting with the North Derbyshire health managers at the Cavendish Hospital Lodge on 13 November 1997. An extension to the Cavendish Hospital for in-patient services was now at an advanced planning stage. The Forum now concentrated on the plans for withdrawal of services from the DRH feeling it important that all services should be withdrawn at the same time to minimise disruption. Discussions took place at Stepping Hill Hospital, Stockport, to clarify progress on reprovision of services. One of the aims of the Forum had been to keep local people informed and, to this end, a public exhibition and presentation was held in the Gym on Friday 20 November 1998. All of the health bodies were again on hand to answer questions, and the plans for the Cavendish extension and the new rheumatology department at Stepping Hill were on display.

Also in attendance was Mike Taylor of the University of Derby, who for some time had followed the activities of the Forum. The new outpatients department was opened at the Cavendish Hospital by the Duke of Devonshire on 25 October 1999 but the closure of the DRH was delayed until July 2000 when the replacement facilities, including those at Cherry Tree Hospital in Stockport for the head-injuries patients, were in place. The closure of the hospital brought to an end the therapeutic use of the Buxton Natural Mineral water, a use which can be traced back to Roman times and for which there is evidence of continuous use from Mediaeval times, perhaps spanning 1000 years - a consequential historical event.

Decorating the dome has occurred on several occasions and is a costly and potentially hazardous business requiring the construction of elaborate scaffolding.

In 1988 a patient, Hilda Baker, who had received a knee joint replacement, organised a sponsored walk from Buxton to Stockport raising £900 for the Buxton branch of the Arthritis and Rheumatism Council for Research. Margery Sherwood, publicity officer for the Buxton branch (extreme right), said that the hospital inspired a great deal of gratitude from people who find they can walk, perhaps for the first time in years, and they set out to raise money for research.

Tea Dance in the Gymnasium in June 1992 for National Music Day and being covered by DRH Television.

The High Peak Health Forum was wound up at a meeting at the Old Hall Hotel on 14 March 2001, and its remaining funds were handed to Arthritis Care. Before the hospital closure a group of local amateur performers joined forces with members of the staff to enact a musical history celebrating the life and work of the hospital. The DRH Musical Association wrote and staged *Dome*, a show based on the Langham & Wells book *The Architect of Victorian Buxton*[160] at the Opera House in April 2000. The £8000 profit from the show was divided equally between four charities, The Arthritis Research Campaign, The Wishbone Trust, The Stroke Association and Headway.

The last public event in the hospital was an ecumenical service conducted by the three hospital chaplains led by Rev. Jim Norton, on 19 July 2000. The service paid tribute to the hospital staff, and was attended by many people who had been connected with the hospital over the past decades. It was fitting that the service took place in a room that had served as dining room, theatre, operating theatre and television studio, in addition to its everyday use as a gymnasium.

Change of Use

After the closure there was much anxiety that the building should find a new tenant as soon as possible and that a new use should be found for it. The sale, on behalf of the NHS Estates, was handled by the Manchester firm of chartered surveyors King Sturge & Co. and suggestions for a use for the building ranged from converting the structure into an indoor shopping mall, the creation of a northern Millennium Dome, a fairground museum, to the outrageous and probably tongue-in-cheek suggestion that the dome area should be used as a car park. One of the earliest to show interest in acquiring the building was the University of Derby whose plan was to turn it into a second campus, thus consolidating a strong presence in the north of the county to match their Kedleston Road campus in Derby. The University, which had merged with with the High Peak College of Further Education in 1998, would move from the Harpur Hill site to the town centre.[161]

DRH Musical Association presents

DOME

a new musical celebrating the life and work of the Devonshire Royal Hospital Buxton

Thursday 13 April
Friday 14 April
Saturday 15 April
7.30pm

Proceeds to charity

Arthritis Research Campaign THE WISHBONE TRUST

STROKE Association HEADWAY

Box Office 01298 72190
Tickets £6.00, £8.00, £10.00
Concessions available

Buxton Opera House

High Peak Theatre Trust Limited. Charity Reg. Number 507354. Supported by High Peak Borough Council

After a carefully mounted campaign the welcome news that the University had succeeded in its bid came in January 2001, with the announcement that the the Department of Health was to transfer the Devonshire to the University at a moderate cost under the, so called, 'gift procedure'. The MP for High Peak, Tom Levitt wrote:

> '... *This decision is absolutely right for Buxton and the High Peak. It opens the way for £2.7m of regeneration funding, £7m of investment in the site and huge opportunities for local people and the local economy...*' [162]

Turning the building from hospital to university is no small project and may be compared with the 1858 conversion from stables to hospital. An expenditure of £8.5 million is deemed to be necessary. The university's vice-chancellor, Professor Roger Waterhouse has said, '...*The challenge will be to create an atmosphere that respects the learning function but also maximises access for the public...*' [163] and, undoubtedly the building will offer a unique university campus.

The conversion will be supported through the Heritage Lottery Fund and it is anticipated that statutory funding bodies will provide £6.5m with the remaining £2m to be found through a public campaign. Though the figures have increased by a considerable order of magnitude, the situation faced by the university and its funding bodies is not dissimilar to that faced by the hospital trustees and the CDCF in 1879. English Heritage has graded the main hospital building as grade 2 starred, and the baths extension as grade 2, which means in essence that any conversion work should not alter the exterior, other than restoring it to its original appearance. The conservation plan and conversion will be overseen by English Heritage and the High Peak Borough Council.

Early work on the conversion has included asbestos removal and the repair and reinstatement of the original pine flooring under the dome. In the hydrotherapy suite original terazzo wall finishes are to be uncovered and repolished and the 1914 baths extension is to keep its two pools as part of a Hydrotherapy Suite. The conversion of the former dining hall, with its original stained-glass windows, will provide a fine new learning centre. Later buildings, provided during the NHS era but no longer required, have been removed to make way for a garden for disabled students. Additional conservation funding will allow the corner roof lanterns (cupolas) and the centre roof lantern glass, some of which is hand-made, to be renovated, and the main entrance gates and perimeter iron railings replaced, as part of a landscape restoration plan.[164]

The campus will provide a base for the University School of Tourism and Hospitality Management, which aims to become a new international centre of excellence. The first director of the University of Derby College, Buxton, Professor David Davies, sees a model for the future of a community university providing a full continuum of learning from basic skills to doctoral research. As this book goes to print, in April 2003, news has arrived of a £4.725m Heritage Lottery grant and it has been announced that the regeneration work will include the introduction of wireless technology to give access to the Internet from any location in the area beneath the dome and the provision of an electronically advanced library for students.

There will be a bistro on the ground floor and a fine dining restaurant on the first floor. Spa, hair and beauty salons will be located on the ground and lower ground floors; all will be training facilities open to the public. A special demonstration lecture theatre for hospitality and catering programmes will have the facility to relay 'masterclasses' live onto a big screen in the dome area.[165]

John Carr's great building now has a further lease of life. After 70 years as stables it began its metamorphosis into medicine, emerging 20 years later as a unique domed hospital. 142 years of specialisation in rheumatic and arthritic disease have seen much learning and advancement of medical knowledge in this place. It is fitting that the resource should now be reshaped as a centre of learning in more diverse fields of academic study.

Epilogue

Upon being given news of the publication of this book, Mrs Elizabeth Snow wrote to the authors:

'...I think R.R. Duke, my great grandfather, would have approved of the new use of the Devonshire Royal Hospital had he been alive now. I am so pleased that you have been able to use some of his drawings...' [166]

The hospital in April 2003 partly scaffolded in preparation for its conversion to University campus.

References and Notes

Chapter 1

1. J. Jones, *The Benefit of the Auncient Bathes of Buckstones*, which cureth most greevous sickness, never before published. (London 1572); Quoted verbatim in T. Short, *The Natural Experimental and Medicinal History of the Mineral Waters of Derbyshire, Lincolnshire and Yorkshire*, London 1734, pp.41.

2. For a fuller account of the visits of Mary Queen of Scots to Buxton see: M. Langham & C. Wells, *A History of the Baths at Buxton, Leek,* 1997, pp. 19-22. Queen Elizabeth was of the opinion that the Earl and Countess of Shrewsbury were making £3-4,000 yearly out of the Peak but Lord Leicester assured her this was untrue. G.R. Batho, *A Calendar of the Shrewsbury and Talbot Papers*, Vol II, London 1971, Vol. F Folio 331.

3. G.R. Batho, *op cit*. Vol. F. Folio 157; E. Axon, *Queen Elizabeth's Tun of Buxton Water,* Paper given to the Buxton Archaeological and Natural History Society' nd. but c.1935/36.

4. S. Glover, *The History and Gazetteer of the County of Derby*, Derby 1833, Pt.l Vol.11 pp.205; E. Axon, *More About Buxton's History, Buxton Advertiser*, 27 October, 3 November 1934; and *Historical Notes on Buxton and its Inhabitants and Visitors*, Paper No. 9. *Buxton Advertiser* 16, 23, 30 March, 6 April 1940; Phyllis Hembry, *The English Spa* 1560-1815, London 1990 pp 31-32.

5. Phyllis Hembry, op. cit. 1990, pp 31; E. Axon, op. cit. Paper no.7. *Buxton Advertiser* 19 & 26 November 1938. Arbella or Arabella Stuart (1575-1632) daughter of Elizabeth Cavendish and granddaughter of Bess of Hardwick.

6. T Fawcett, *Bath Administer'd, Corporation Affairs in the 18th Century Spa*, Bath 2001, pp. 60-61; Phyllis Hembry op. cit. 1990, pp.32.

7. T.Short, *op. cit.*, 1734, pp. 43; M. Langham & C. Wells, *A History of the Baths at Buxton*, Leek, 1997, pp. 26.

8. Quoted in E. Axon, *op. cit*. Paper no. 8. *Buxton Advertiser* 2, 9, 23 December 1939; D. Defoe, *A Tour through the Whole Island of Great Britain*, (P.N. Furbank & W.R. Owens eds.) London, 1991 pp. 246.

9. T. Fawcett, *op. cit*. pp. 61-62; G. Davis & Penny Bonsall, *Bath - A New History*, Keele 1996, pp. 49

10. Denman, J. MD, *Observations on Buxton Water*, London 1793 and 1801. Dr Denman says: '...[the bath] till lately, has been shamefully and unwarrantably neglected, and in great disorder...' pp. 45 1801 Edn.

11. W. Bray, *Sketch of a Tour into Derbyshire and Yorkshire*, London 1783, pp. 232.

12. Bott, *A Description of Buxton and the Adjacent Country or the New Guide etc.*, Manchester 1795, pp. 11-12.

13. The rules were reprinted in the preface to the Buxton Bath Charity Annual Report 1865.

14. A Jewitt, *The History of Buxton*, London 1811, pp 65-66; D. Orme, *The New Buxton Guide*, Macclesfield 1823, pp 16-22; *Buxton Bath Charity Annual Reports*, 1831, 1836, 1840, 1850, 1854; J.A. Pearson, *Reports of Cases Treated at the Buxton Bath Charity and Devonshire Hospital*, Liverpool 1861, passim.

15. C. Scudamore (Sir) MD., *The Analysis and Medical Account of the Tepid Springs of Buxton*, London, 1833, pp. 34-36.

16. R. Ward (Rev), *A Guide to the Peak of Derbyshire*, Birmingham, 1827. Reprinted Didsbury, Manchester, 1972, pp. 172-74

17. J.E. Todmorden, 'On my visit to the Devonshire Hospital' Buxton April 26,1866. Buxton Local Studies Library

18. A.B. Granville, *The Spas of England Vol. 2. The Midlands*, London 1841. Reprinted Bath 1971, pp.43; W. Adam, *Gem of the Peak*, London, 1843, pp. 27-30.

19. W.H. Robertson, *A Handbook to the Peak of Derbyshire*, London 1854, pp. 162.

20. Robertson, *Op.Cit*. 1854, pp. 169-70.

21. Percy, Sir Hugh, third Duke of Northumberland, (1785-1847), he was Lord Lieutenant of Ireland 1829-30. *D.N.B.* Concise version, Oxford, 1948; Sir Edward Bulwer Lytton Bart (1803-1873), noted novelist and playwright. He took several courses of hydropathic treatment and published *Confessions of a Water Cure patient* in 1847; Viscount Combermere (1773-1865) had a distinguished military career. A Privy Councillor and Constable of the Tower of London, he was a regular visitor to Buxton. M. Langham, *Buxton - A People's History*, Lancaster, 2001, pp. 118-19 & 50 footnote.

22. *Buxton Bath Charity Annual Report*, 1854; The Bath Hospital at Harrogate was rebuilt on a larger scale in 1889 and re-named The Royal Bath Hospital and Rawson Convalescent Home. It could accommodate 150 patients. Phyllis Hembry, *British Spas from 1815 to the Present*, London 1997, pp.137 & 168; The Harrogate Medical Society, *Spa Treatment*, Harrogate c.1930, pp.37.

23. Letter and accounts of the Buxton Bath Charity Building Fund dated 2 May 1857 by EW Wilmot, Langham & Wells Papers, Buxton (Devonshire Hospital Box)

24. Supplement to the preface of the *Annual report of Devonshire Hospital and Buxton Bath Charity 1900*, Duke/DH/1 47, The Duke Papers Buxton; M. Langham & C. Wells, *The Architect of Victorian Buxton*, Matlock, 1996, pp l41-42 & 186; Henry Currey's hospital plan was subsequently used for the Wye House Asylum on Corbar Road which was built in 1859-60 and run by the medical family of Dicksons as a mental hospital. In 1912 it became the Cavendish School for Girls.

Chapter 2

25. H.Colvin, *A Biographical Dictionary of British Architects 1600-1840*, London 1995, pp2l 7.

26. W. Adam, *The Gem of the Peak*, 4th edn. London 1845 pp 314.

27. E. Rhodes, *Peak Scenery*, London 1924, pp 101-2

28. I. Hall, *Georgian Buxton*, Matlock 1984. pp 28; G A Cooke, *Topographical and Statistical Description of the County of Derbyshire*, London 1830, pp54

29. Pigot & Co. *Commercial Directory for Derbyshire*, 1835. Facsimile Edn. Matlock 1976, p 25.

30. S. Bagshaw, *A History, Gazetteer and Directory of Derbyshire*, Sheffield 1846, pp. 434. 31

31. *Freebody's Directory of the Towns of Derbyshire, 1852*; White's Directory of Derbyshire 1857.

32 The Turner & Duke partnership had been responsible for masons work on the new road from the Quadrant to the Great Stables and were also paid a total of £241 for alterations and additions to the Crescent stables in 1857. In 1859 R.R. Duke s building business did further conversion work, being paid £110 for converting sheds into stables. M. Langham & C. Wells. *op.cit* 1996.

33. Plan of 1858, showing the ground floor layout with pencilled alterations for the later (1879-82) conversions. Photocopy plan, Langham & Wells Papers.

34. *Devonshire Hospital and Buxton Bath Charity, Annual Report*, 1911. pp l2.

35. Devonshire Hospital Conversion plans and specification 1 Jan and 6 March 1858, D4508/31 /1-9, Derbyshire Record Office, Matlock; Royal Commission on the Historic Monuments of England. 'Devonshire Royal Hospital', February 1997, passim. Crown Copyright.

36. O.S. Map Buxton 1878

37. *Buxton Office 1856 to 1889*, (A record of informal discussions with people making requests of theDuke of Devonshire's agent) Folio, Devonshire Collections, Chatsworth. Currey & Co. of Great George Street, Westminster were solicitors and financiers to the Devonshire Cavendish family.

38. Indenture and plan 1868 and 1878, D4508/1 2/21 Derbyshire Record Office, Matlock.

39. Structural Perspectives, *'Historic building report and Assessment of the Dome at the Devonshire Royal Hospital, Buxton'*, Halifax, 2002, passim. The Concert Hall in the Pavilion Gardens built for the Buxton Improvements Company.

40. M. Langham & C. Wells. *The Architect of Victorian Buxton, A Biography of Robert Rippon Duke*, Matlock 1996.

41. *Buxton Advertiser*, August 17 1867

42. A term meaning 'dead hand' part of Mediaeval law designed to safeguard income due to the manorial lord where changes in land ownership took place. It was probably used by the duke's solicitor to safeguard income from the stables. J. Richardson, *The Local Historian's Encyclopedia*, New Barnet 1993, pp. 24.

43. Devonshire Royal Hospital, Minutes of Board Trustees 3 September 1870. (Now at the Derbyshire Record Office, Matlock)

44. N. Longmate. *The Hungry Mills*, London. 1978

45. Charges at this time were normally £1 .l0s. for three weeks after which a charge of l0s. was made for as long as the patient remained on the ward.

46 See chapter three for a description of the funding arrangements and recommendations.

47. Robert Rippon Duke was also trustee of the Devonshire Hospital and Buxton Bath Charity from 1859 to 1909.

48. R.R. Duke, *Devonshire Hospital,* privately published pamphlet, 1 October 1902, Duke/DH/010, The Duke Papers, Buxton

49. *The Engineer,* 17 September 1886. *Engineering* 17 September 1886, obituaries of Roland Mason Ordish. *D.N.B.* Concise version, Oxford, 1948.

50. Ashworth to Robertson, 11 August 1879. Devonshire Hospital Minute Book, 1879-1894.

51. Structural Perspectives. *op. cit.* see pp. 9 & 10 for a description of the partnerships of Richard, John and Henry Rankin in Liverpool.

52. *Engineering* magazine *op. cit.*

53. Structural Perspectives. op. cit. R.M. Ordish was involved in the design of the Great Exhibition building, (the Crystal Palace) in 1851 and, amongst many important structures, designed the roofs for the St Pancras, London and Enoch Square Station, Glasgow and other stations, and the Albert Hall dome roof (1867-71). *D.N.B.* Concise version, Oxford, 1948; The Engineer *op. cit.*

54. R.R. Duke, 'An Autobiography' 1902.

55. R.R. Duke, 1902 *op. cit.*

56. *Builder Magazine* 10 July 1880

57. Devonshire Hospital Building committee minutes 9 December 1880

58. Devonshire Hospital Building committee minutes 5 & 14 February 1881

59. Devonshire Hospital Building committee minutes 2 May 1881

60. Letter from Samuel Warburton to Mr J Taylor, Secretary of the Devonshire Hospital trustees dated 4 March 1881. Devonshire Hospital papers (Now at the Derbyshire Record Office, Matlock)

61. Special meeting of Devonshire Hospital Building Committee 14 March 1881

62. *Buxton Advertiser*, August 2nd 1882; Fieldwork 10 February 2003

63. *Buxton Advertiser,* July 9th 1881

64. R.R. Duke's notebook, Duke/DH/002, p. 4. The Duke Papers, Buxton.

65. *Engineer* Magazine 27January 1882.

66. *Buxton Advertiser,* 31 December 1881

Chapter 3

67. M. Langham, *Buxton A People's History*, Lancaster, 2001, pp. 114

68. R.R. Duke's notebook, Duke/DH/002, pp.34, The Duke Papers, Buxton.

69. *Buxton Advertiser* 11 October 1884 and 8 May 1897, the quarterly reports of the Devonshire Hospital & Buxton Bath Charity.

70. 'Proposal for the erection of a portico and clock tower' appeal document issued 22 March 1880. Duke/DH/67, The Duke Papers, Buxton

71. *Buxton Advertiser*, 6 August 1881. The architect records the cost of the tower at £1034. R.R. Duke's notebook, Duke/DH/002, *op. cit.*

72. Royal Commission on the Historical Monuments of England, Draft report, the Devonshire Royal Hospital, Feb. 1997, pp.11.

73. Handwritten note by R.R. Duke, late 1882, ML/H823, The Langham Papers, Buxton.

74. Minutes of the Buxton Local Board, 20 September 1885, Dl 323 Derbyshire Record Office, Matlock R.R. Duke, 'The early stages of Buxton's progress', 1906. Privately published pamphlet, Duke/DH/011, The Duke Papers, Buxton.

76. *The British Medical Journal*, 17 March 1883, pp. 539-40. The word used by the correspondent is a variant spelling of 'Brobdingnagian' which derives from from Jonathan Swift's *Gulliver's Travels* where, in the fabulous region of Brobdingnag, everything was gigantic. *Chambers 20th Century Dictionary*, edn. c.1950.

77. *The British Medical Journal*, March/April 1883, pp. 691-92.

78. R.R. Duke, *Devonshire Hospital*, Buxton 1st October 1902. Private pamphlet. Duke/DH1OA, The Duke Papers, Buxton.

79. For more detailed account, M. Langham & C. Wells, *The Architect of Victorian Buxton*, Matlock, 1996, ch.8.

80. Printed letter R.R. Duke to the management committee c. 1905, ML/H/819 The Langham Papers, Buxton

81. Devonshire Hospital Building Committee Minute Book, 6 March 1884; Management Committee, 25 March 1884, Derbyshire Record Office, Matlock.

82. R.R. Duke, *Devonshire Hospital,* Buxton 1st October 1902. Private pamphlet. Duke/DH1OA, The Duke Papers, Buxton.

83. R.R. Duke, *Devonshire Hospital and Buxton Bath Charity*, private pamphlet, c.1897, Duke/DH/009, The Duke Papers, Buxton.

84. Ground and chamber plan of extensions, plan no. 8. Duke/DH/98, The Duke Papers, Buxton; Ground plan in *The Builder,* 3 December 1881.

85. Jubilee Accident Wards, Proof Rules and Regulations, 25 Jan 1900, Duke/DH/65. The Duke Papers, Buxton.

86. *Buxton Advertiser*, 14 May 1898

87. R.R. Duke, 'Accident Wards' manuscript record, Duke/DH/146, the Duke Papers Buxton

88. Instructions to Counsel to Advise' (Draft) November 1904, Duke/DH/1 455; Letter 22 November 1905, W. Stevenson, hospital secretary, to R.R. Duke, Duke/DH/144; Printed letter R.R. Duke to the Committee of Management,c.1905, ML/H815, The Langham Papers, Buxton; Legal papers, D4508/1 5/1, Derbyshire Record Office, Matlock.

89. *Devonshire Hospital & Buxton Bath Charity Annual Report*, 1914, ML/1 39, The Langham Papers, Buxton

90. See for example the *Buxton Herald* 16 July 1902.

91. Handwritten record by R.R. Duke, folio, Duke/DH/140, The Langham Papers, Buxton.

92. M. Langham & C. Wells, 1996 *op.cit.* pp. 181-82; Notes by R.R. Duke 20.02.1891 on hot water warming apparatus, ML/H/828, The Langham Papers, Buxton

93. M. Langham & C. Wells, 1996, *op.cit.* pp. 200.

94. Henry Spalding report to the Management Committee, 31 October 1903, Duke/DH/007, The Duke Papers, Buxton

95. Minutes of Management Committee, 1887-93, D4508/1 0/2, Derbyshire Record Office, Matlock

96. M.Langham & C. Wells, 1996 *op.cit.* pp. 202-02

97. Confidential report by F.K. Dickson & H.A. Hubbersty 13 September 1899, Duke/DH/148; Confidential report by R.R. Duke, 7 December 1899, Duke/DH/149, The Duke Papers, Buxton.

98. *Devonshire Hospital & Buxton Bath Charity Annual Report*, 1914 op.cit. pp. 51.

99. Letter S. Pettit to S.M. Smith 20 June 1896, Duke/DH/27, The Duke Papers, Buxton

100. Postcard, F.M. Little to S.M. Smith 8 October 1898, Duke/DH/31, The Duke Papers, Buxton

101. *Devonshire Hospital & Buxton Bath Charity Annual Report*, 1914 op.cit.; 1901 & 1902, Buxton Local Studies Library.

102. Notebook of R.R. Duke, Duke/DH/002, The Duke Papers, Buxton

103. *Devonshire Hospital & Buxton Bath Charity Annual Report*, 1899, D4508/1 0/4 Reports 1894-1900 Derbyshire Record Office, Matlock

104. See M. Langham , op.cit. 2002, pp. 244.

105. *Buxton Advertiser*, 1 January 1903.

106. M. Langham, 2001 *op. cit.* ch. 5.; M. Langham & C. Wells, *Six Buxton Gentlemen*, Buxton, 1995, pp. 11-15.

107. Architect's notebook, Duke/DH/002. The Duke Papers, Buxton.

108. Devonshire Hospital printed copy.of Sub-committee Meeting 17 September 1896, Duke/DH/64; Copy letter R.R.Duke to J. Taylor, secretary, 6 April 1895, Duke/DH/68. Plans, Duke/DH 127-132. The Duke Papers, Buxton.

109. Devonshire Hospital House Committee minutes, 1 May 1890; 5 March 1892

110. *Buxton Advertiser*, June 1899.

111. Architect's notebook, Duke/DH/002. The Duke Papers, Buxton.

112. *Buxton Advertiser*, 7 Jan 1905

113. *Devonshire Hospital Annual Report*, 1914. pp 41

114. *Kelly's Derbyshire 1939*; Correspondence Dr C.W. Buckley and the Hospital secretary, D4508/28/6, Derbyshire Record Office, Matlock

Chapter 4

115. M. Langham & C. Wells, *William Radford Bryden F.R.I.B.A. A short biography.* Bulletin no.28 Autumn 1999. Buxton Archaeological and Natural History Society.

116. Devonshire Hospital, Plan of Proposed New Baths, 1913, D4508/31/2, Derbyshire Record Office, Matlock.

117. Royal Commission on the Historical Monuments of England, *Historic Building Report.* DRH. February 1997. pp.12.

118. Royal Commission, Op. cit. 1997, pp. 11; *Devonshire Royal Hospital Handbook*, December 1990, pp.4.

119. *Buxton Advertiser*, October 2002. 50 years ago column.

120. *Annual Report of the Devonshire Hospital* Year ending 31 December 1914. p 22

121. *Annual Report of the Devonshire Hospital* Year ending 31 December 1919.

122. J. Leach, *The Book of Buxton.* Buckinghamshire 1987

123. Photocopy of undated poem written by Pte F C Welsh. R.A.M.C. of Blackburn. Langham & Wells collection, Buxton.

124. Vera Brittain, *Testament of Youth.* Fontana 1980. pp 164

125. Committee of the Research Society of the Devonshire Hospital. *The Natural, Thermal and Chalybeate Waters of Buxton - A brief account of their action and uses*, Buxton 1924, passim.

126. C.W. Buckley, *Arthritis in the Spa Hospitals*, British Medical Journal 17 June 1933

127. *Devonshire Hospital Annual Report* 1914.op cit pp 20

128. R. Porter, *The Greatest Benefit To Mankind.* London 1997. pp 459-460.

129. *Devonshire Hospital Annual Report* 1914.op cit pp.27

130. *Devonshire Hospital Annual Report* Year ending December 1919

131. *Devonshire Hospital Annual Report* Year ending December 1930.

132. The staff dining room was for the exclusive use of nursing sisters until the mid 1960s.

133. *Devonshire Hospital Annual Report*, Year ending December 1945 pp 11

134. *Devonshire Hospital Centenary Guide*, 1859-1959 pp 11.

135. *Buxton Advertiser*, 18 September 1942

136. *Devonshire Hospital, All through the Years*, 1937, ML/140 Langham & Wells Papers, Buxton

137. *Devonshire Hospital Anpual Report* 1914 pp.41.

138. J. Leach *op. cit.* 1987

139. M. Langham, *Buxton, A People's History.* Lancaster 2001.

140. Pendennis Nurses Accommodation, papers D4508/32/4, Derbyshire Record Office, Matlock.

141. M. Langham op. cit. 2001. pp 215. M. Langham & C. Wells, 1997, op. cit. pp 83.

142. The Hot & Natural Baths were purchased in 1904 by Buxton Corpn. for £55,000. M. Langham & C. Wells, 1997 op. cit. pp 74.

143. Papers on collaboration with the Empire Rheumatism Council, 1937, D4508/47/1, Derbyshire Record Office, Matlock.

144. J. Leach op. cit. 1987. pp 78

145. More latterly the Buxton and Cavendish hospitals were managed by the Community Health Care Service NHS Trust and at the present time by the High Peak & Dales Primary Care NHS Trust.

146. Vera Brittain op cit 1980 pp. 170

147. 'A scheme for the provision of hospital and specialist services at the Rheumatism Centre, Buxton. April 1947' lists, in sect. 12, a proposed operating theatre block at the Devonshire Royal Hospital - which suggests no operating theatre in use at the time.

148. Correspondence with Mr J M Laughton retired Consultant Orthopaedic Surgeon. July 2003

149. M. Bentley, M. Langham & C. Wells, *Buxton from the Board Collection*, Stroud 1999.

150. *Devonshire Hospital Annual Report* year ending 1939

151. M. Langham *op cit.* 2001. pp. 114 & 119

152. Nicola Clemence, *Physiotherapy - A hundred years of medical rubbing*, Norfolk & Norwich Institute for Medical Education Journal Vol 10. Autumn 1995 pp3I-36.

153. *Devonshire Hospital Annual Report* year ending 1904.

154. *Devonshire Hospital Annual Report* Year ending 1932. pp22.

155. For a more detailed explanation of treatments, M.Langham & C. Wells, *A history of the Baths at Buxton,* Leek 1997

156. The group exercise sessions were originally 'compered' by two Remedial Gymnasts who had received their training during military service in the war years.

157. J. Lea. *Reach for my Countryside.* Leek 1999

158. Stockport Health Commission, Public Consultation Document on the Future of Services Provided at The Devonshire Royal Hospital Buxton , Dec. 1995; Rawlinson Kelly Whittlestone, High Peak Hospitals Estates review, June 1995.

159. REMAP: Rehabilitation Engineering Movement Advisory Panels, a movement originated by Teeside engineer, Pat Johnson, with a panel of professional engineers and handymen from staff at ICI Billingham. They started designing and building aids for disabled people. Panels were soon formed elsewhere. The Buxton panel was one of the first, and met monthly at the D R H to discuss cases which had been referred for help. *The High Peak Courier*, January 1987.

160. M. Langham & C. Wells, *The Architect of Victorian Buxton - A biography of Robert Rippon Duke*, Matlock 1996.

161. *The Guardian,* 5 April 1999; The Times 5 April 1999.

162. Email, T. Levitt to M. Langham January 2001

163. D. Ward, Students to revive spa town's fortunes Guardian Unlimited website, www.guardian .co.uklarchive

164. *Devonshire Echo*, issues 01, September and 02, November, 2002

165. *Buxton Advertiser*, 2 April 2003.

166. Correspondence E. Snow to MJ Langham 11 March 2003

Appendix

The 104th Annual Report of the Devonshire Hospital and Buxton Bath Charity for the year 1914

MEDICAL REPORT

316 beds were available in the hospital

Of the 4364 cases under treatment during 1914: In-patients numbered 3902 : Out-patients numbered 462

Rheumatism

	Males	Females	Total
Acute Rheumatism	10	11	21
Subacute Rheumatism	440	324	764
Chronic Articular Rheumatism	160	7	167
Fibrositis and Muscular Rheumatism	412	252	664
			1616

Gout

	Males	Females	Total
Acute Gout	59	3	62
Chronic Gout	114	14	128
			190

Other Forms of Arthritis

	Males	Females	Total
Infective Arthritis	280	323	603
Chronic Infective Arthritis (Rheumatoid)	118	204	322
Osteo-arthritis	271	313	584
Traumatic Arthritis	4	2	6
Tubercular Arthritis	2	0	2
			1517

Diseases not included in the preceding main groups

Diseases of the Nervous System

	Males	Females	Total
Sciatica	386	60	446
Other forms of Neuritis	81	67	148
Hemiplegia	11	4	15
Tabes Dorsalis	3	1	4
Neurasthenia	12	14	26
Disseminated Sclerosis	7	3	10
Lateral Sclerosis	1	0	1
Spastic Paraplegia	8	2	10
Transverse Myelitis	5	1	6
Anterior Polyomyelitis	2	2	4
Chorea	0	3	3
Paralysis Agitans	1	0	1
Facial Paralysis	0	1	1
Metatarsalgia	0	1	1
Pleurodynia	1	0	1
			677

	Males	Females	Total

Diseases of the Digestive System

	Males	Females	Total
Dyspepsia	13	0	13
Mucous Colitis	0	1	1
			14

Diseases of the Blood and Ductless Glands

	Males	Females	Total
Anaemia	0	1	1
Pernicious Anaemia	1	0	1
Exophthalmic Goitre	0	1	1
Tonsillitis	3	0	3
			6

Diseases of Blood Vessels

	Males	Females	Total
Varicose Veins	1	0	1
Intermittent Claudication	1	0	1
			2

Diseases of the Heart (Non-Rheumatic)

	Males	Females	Total
Myocarditis	2	0	2
Endocarditis	3	0	3
Stokes-Adams Disease	1	0	1

Cardiac Debility	6	0	6
			12

Disease of the Genito-Urinary System

Chronic Nephritis	2	0	2
			2

Diseases of the Skin

Furunculosis	1	0	1
Pruritus	1	0	1
Psoriasis	1	1	2
Eczema	0	1	1
			5

Diseases of Vertebral Column

Spondylitis Deformans	2	0	2
Spinal Curvature	1	1	2
Spinal Caries	0	2	2
			6

Constitutional Diseases

Convalescents (Various)	15	0	15
			15

Intoxications

Plumbism	1	2	3
Chronic Mercurial Poisining	1	0	1
Alcoholic Neuritis	2	1	3
Diabetic Neuritis	0	1	1
			8

	Males	Females	Total
Diseases of Respiratory System			
Acute Bronchitis	3	0	3
Chronic Bronchitis	5	0	5
Pleurisy	1	0	1
			9

Diseases of Organs of Special Sense

Nystagmus	1	0	1
Meniere's Disease	1	0	1
Otitis Media	2	0	2
			4

Trophic Neurosis

Adiposa Dolorosa		1	1
			1

Diseases of Bones and Joints

Tubercular Synovitis	1	0	1
Tubercular Hip	9	6	15
Tubercular Spine	0	3	3
Charcot's Disease	1	0	1
			20

Surgical Cases and Deformities

Pes Planus	12	8	20
Subacromial Bursitis	10	1	11
Sprains and Traumatic Synovitis	16	2	18
Bullet and Shrapnel wounds	138	0	138
Fractures	26	1	27
Injuries to Back	18	0	18
Other Injuries	22	0	22
Displaced Semilunar Cartilage	4	0	4
Perinaeal Abscess	1	0	1
Interstitial Hernia	1	0	1
			260

		Total	4364

D.K. Parkes, M.B., Ch.B., Liverp., House Surgeon

Harold Fairclough, M.B., B.S., Dunelm, Assistant House Surgeon

Index